John Avanzini
...ers Your Questions
...ut Biblical Economics

by

John Avanzini

Harrison House
Tulsa, OK

*John Avanzini Answers Your Questions
About Biblical Economics*

ISBN: 0-89274-906-7

First Printing: 170,000 copies

Unless otherwise indicated, all Scripture quotations
are taken from the *King James Version* of the Bible.

Verses marked **TLB** are taken from *The Living Bible*.
Copyright 1971. Used by permission of Tyndale
House Publishers, Inc., Wheaton, Illinois 60189. All
rights reserved.

For emphasis, the author has placed selected words
from the Bible quotations in italics.

Harrison House
P.O. Box 35035
Tulsa, OK 74153

We dedicate this book to
Patrick Ondrey,
our faithful son in the Lord.

John & Pat Avanzini

Contents

Introduction

Answering the questions of God's people is a legitimate biblical function of the five-fold ministry (Ephesians 4:11). Scripture tells us the Apostle Paul answered people's questions.

> Now about those questions you asked in your last letter: my answer is. . . .
> 1 Corinthians 7:1 TLB

I thank God for the new interest Christians are showing in getting biblical answers to the questions of life. It is evident that the true children of God have grown tired of the canned answers they have been receiving from so-called religious leaders. God's people are now insisting on fresh manna from His Word. They want straight answers, backed up by Scripture.

In this book, you will find my answers to the twenty most-asked questions about money. They range from questions about the tithe all the way to whether or not a Christian should use a credit card.

The answers on these pages are not the mere thoughts of John Avanzini. To the best of my ability, I have based them on God's Word. If I had not, they would be of little value to you, for the Scripture says:

> All scripture is given by inspiration of God, and is profitable for doctrine, for reproof, for correction, for instruction in righteousness:

> **That the man of God may be perfect,**
> **throughly furnished unto all good works.**
> **2 Timothy 3:16,17**

I have tried my best to mix sound biblical interpretation with practical, common sense, for Scripture warns us to avoid Bible teachers who give great discourses on unimportant trivia.

> **. . . charge . . . that they teach no other**
> **doctrine,**
> **Neither give heed to fables and endless**
> **genealogies, which minister questions, rather**
> **than godly edifying. . . .**
> **1 Timothy 1:3,4**

In selecting which questions to deal with, I have avoided the foolish ones, for the Word of God warns against answering them.

> **. . . avoid foolish questions, and genealogies,**
> **and contentions, and strivings about the law; for**
> **they are unprofitable and vain.**
> **Titus 3:9**

Before you begin to read the contents of this book, please allow me one courtesy. If, for some reason, you do not agree with some of my answers, I most humbly ask you not to judge me too harshly. I have not written this book to divide us, but simply to answer your questions. Now, let me begin.

Why should I obey the Bible about how I spend my money?

Recently a man from Miami wrote, "Why should I let the Bible tell me how I am supposed to spend my money? I feel that if I earned it, I ought to have the right to spend it the way I want."

I would like you to consider some facts before you agree with this person's conclusion. As you know, it is important for Christians to look at the Word of God as it pertains to *every part* of their lives. We must do this because the Bible is God's word of instruction to those He has saved. We are told that it is to be:

> . . . a lamp unto my feet, and a light unto my path.
>
> **Psalm 119:105**

Your Money Is Important to God's Will

Since God's Word shows us how to live the Christian life, and seeing that the way we use our money is a large part of our lives, it is imperative that we allow the Bible to guide us in the spending of our money. In fact, the Bible must be the final authority in all of our money matters, for the very money we earn comes to us through God's power.

That's right! Money comes to us by God's power, and not by our own.

> . . . thou shalt remember the Lord thy God:
> for it is he that giveth thee power to get wealth. . . .
> **Deuteronomy 8:18**

There is no question about it. You did invest your time and energy in earning your money. However, you must remember that you are not like the children of this world. You have been "bought with a price . . ." (1 Corinthians 6:20). You are no longer your own.

> . . . old things are passed away; behold, all
> things are become new.
> **2 Corinthians 5:17**

Yes, you did spend your time to get an education. You have worked hard to develop your own business. You have vigorously participated in getting every dollar you have. However, if you are in Christ, your finances have come to you through a process totally different from the method of the world. The Bible says you receive your money through a supernatural miracle power that God has placed in your hands. Not only did He give you the supernatural power to get your wealth, He was also careful to tell you exactly how He wants you to spend it.

Please notice that in the same verse that tells of our God-given power to get wealth, God also tells us why we have that power.

> . . . [He] giveth thee power to get wealth,
> that he may establish his covenant which he
> sware unto thy fathers, as it is this day.
> **Deuteronomy 8:18**

Let's start looking at it God's way. He has given you the power to obtain wealth for the specific purpose of funding the end-time harvest. If the Christians of this end time don't soon come into an understanding of this truth, some great problems will arise in the future.

God Will File Embezzlement Charges

Please note that I am not speaking only of the problems that a lack of funds will cause. I am also speaking of the problems the Christians of our era will face when they stand in the judgment of God.

As most of you know, it is impossible to have a proper judgment without filing an indictment against the accused. With all of my heart, I believe the charge God will bring against most Christians will be that of *embezzlement*. Simply stated, God will accuse them of taking that which belonged to Him, and using it for their own selfish purposes.

Seek Out God's Purposes

Since your power to get money comes from God, it is important for you to seek out carefully how He wants you to spend it. It is obvious from Scripture that you should spend a part of everything you earn to fulfill God's purpose. You will never be able to receive full satisfaction and happiness from the money you earn until you have met God's expectations for it. Remember, sorrow-free money comes from God's own hand.

**The blessing of the Lord, it maketh rich,
and he addeth no sorrow with it.
Proverbs 10:22**

Now, that's what I call good news! However, please notice that something totally different happens to the person who gathers money for the wrong purposes.

> **But they that will be rich fall into temptation and a snare, and into many foolish and hurtful lusts, which drown men in destruction and perdition.**
> **1 Timothy 6:9**

The Scripture is clear. Money gained for the wrong reason eventually leads to much sorrow and eternal damnation.

God Has a Right to Speak

With these things said, it becomes evident that God has a right to speak to you about how you spend your money. First, He has that right because He gives you the power to get wealth. Second, if you gather and disburse money improperly, it will be a big detriment to your happiness and well being.

Remember, God has a purpose for every dollar He places in your hands.

Become a Steward

I must say one last thing about this subject. It is important for every Christian to acknowledge that the Bible is the only authorized manual for living the proper Christian life. As you read God's Word, it will become evident that He doesn't look upon you as a proprietor. He looks upon you as His steward. As we all know, Christian stewards handle God's money, not their own.

Now don't let this truth trouble you, for *God always generously rewards His faithful stewards.*

> **His lord said unto him, Well done, thou good and faithful servant [steward]: thou hast been faithful over a few things, I will make thee ruler over many things. . . .**
> **Matthew 25:21**

God wants you to use a part of everything He puts in your hands for your personal needs and pleasure. He is a just Master, and He would not ask you to be His steward without properly attending to your needs and wants.

Why should you obey the Bible about how you spend your money? God has given you power to obtain your wealth. If you don't follow His instructions as to how you spend it, your money will cause you sorrow, and it can never bring you satisfaction.

Question 2

Are tithes and offerings the same?

I continue to be amazed at the number of people who are confused between the tithe and an offering. Even some ministers of the gospel mistakenly interchange these two words. One Sunday they may say, "It's time to take up the tithe." The next week it may be, "It's time to receive the offering."

Tithing is not just another word for the Sunday offering. The tithe and the offering are two different things.

First, *the tithe is always a specified percentage of a person's increase. The offering is always a discretionary amount.*

The Tithe Is 10 Percent

It would be wrong to say, "Well, I think I'll tithe $20.00 this month," for the amount of the tithe is unchangable. It is always 10 percent of your increase. When you take time to read what the Scripture actually has to say concerning the percentage of the tithe, there is no room left for doubt. When Abraham returned home with the spoils from his victory over the five kings, in Genesis Scripture says he tithed.

> **. . . And he gave him tithes of all.**
> **Genesis 14:20**

When the writer of Hebrews gave an account of the same event in the New Testament, he said Abraham gave 10 percent.

> **. . . Abraham gave a tenth part of all. . . .**
> **Hebrews 7:2**

When you compare these two accounts, it becomes obvious that when the Bible speaks of the tithe, it is speaking of 10 percent of the increase.

The Offering Is a Discretionary Amount

The giver always determines the amount of his offering. The New Testament states that it isn't any set amount. Paul made this absolutely clear when he explained to the saints at Corinth how they should give.

> **Every one must make up his own mind as to how much he should give. Don't force anyone to give more than he really wants to, for cheerful givers are the ones God prizes.**
> **2 Corinthians 9:7 TLB**

The Apostle Paul said that an offering should reflect the heart of the giver, and each individual Christian must decide how much he will give. The one who receives the offering is to use absolutely no pressure, for cheerful givers add a special dimension of pleasure to God in each offering.

Be sure to keep it straight. Tithes and offerings are two completely different things. The tithe is a fixed percentage of your increase. The offering is a flexible amount regulated by your love for God.

There is another important difference between the tithe and the offering. *The tithe is a trust relationship. The offering is a gift relationship.*

The Tithe Is a Trust

Let me illustrate the trust relationship of the tithe. Suppose you were my steward in charge of caring for my property, and I gave you $100.00 per day for expenses and safekeeping. Let's say I told you I wanted you to set aside 10 percent ($10.00) of every $100.00, and save it for me. You were not to spend it under any circumstances. You were to make sure it would be available to me whenever I wanted it.

Suppose I also told you that with the remaining 90 percent, you could buy food, clothing, and anything else you might need, as long as you continued faithfully to set aside 10 percent for my account.

That would be a *trust relationship.* This illustration is easy for a tither to understand, for it is parallel to the relationship he shares with his God.

Here is an example from my own life. My house has a lock on the front door. However, all of my trusted children have keys to that lock. Because they have developed a trust relationship with me, I have given them access to all of my personal belongings.

In that same way, when you establish a trust relationship with God through your faithful tithing, He will give you access to heaven by opening the windows.

> Bring ye all the tithes into the storehouse, that there may be meat in mine house, and prove me now herewith, saith the Lord of hosts, if I will not *open you the windows of heaven, and pour you out a blessing.* ...
>
> Malachi 3:10

An Offering Is a Gift

The relationship you create with God through your offerings is much different, for it is a *gift relationship.* An offering is a present from you to God.

If you were to give me a present, I would have no right to say, "Wait a minute. This gift just isn't enough!" or, "I think I need to see your financial statement, because this gift looks a little skimpy."

A gift is just that. It's a gift. It doesn't come forth by command *from the receiver,* but it comes forth *from the heart of the giver.*

Your offering should always be a statement of your love and gratitude. Your tithe is always a statement of your obedience to God's command.

Taken or Given

There is yet another difference between tithes and offerings. Scripture usually speaks of the priests *taking the tithe.*

> ... the priesthood, have a commandment to
> *take tithes of the people.* ...
> **Hebrews 7:5**

On the other hand, a minister does not take an offering, but *receives it.* It is clear from Scripture that we are to *pay* our tithe and *bring* our offering.

> ... [Levi] *paid* tithes in Abraham.
> **Hebrews 7:9**

> Therefore if thou *bring* thy gift to the altar. ...
> **Matthew 5:23**

The Key and the Seed

Let's quickly look at one more difference between the tithe and the offering. Your tithe is a *key,* while your offering is a *seed.*

The *tithe is a key* because it opens the windows of heaven for you. Remember, God's Word clearly directs you to:

> **Bring ye all the tithes into the storehouse,**
> **that there may be meat in mine house, and prove**
> **me now herewith, saith the Lord of hosts, if I will**
> **not *open you the windows of heaven.* ...**
> **Malachi 3:10**

Your *offering is a seed.* The Apostle Paul said that when we give money to God's work, it becomes more than a non-living metal such as silver or gold. God actually turns it into a living seed.

> **But remember this — if you give little, you**
> **will get little. A farmer who plants just a few**

seeds will get only a small crop, but if he plants much, he will reap much.

Every one must make up his own mind as to how much he should give. Don't force anyone to give more than he really wants to, for cheerful givers are the ones God prizes.

2 Corinthians 9:6,7 TLB

Remember, tithes and offerings are not the same. Your tithe *belongs to God,* but your offering *is yours to give.* The tithe is essential to your having an open heaven. The offering is an expression of your love for God.

Question 3

Should I tithe on my net income
or on my gross income?

One of the questions people ask me most often concerning biblical economics is, "How do I calculate my tithe? Does the Lord expect me to pay my tithe on the amount of money I receive after my payroll deductions, or am I supposed to tithe on the total amount of my earnings before any deductions are taken out? Brother John, which is the right way?"

Maybe a simple illustration will help you better understand what is actually involved. Let's say you earn $10.00 an hour and regularly work a forty-hour week. Your gross income would be forty hours times $10.00 per hour, or $400.00.

If the withholding (taxes, etc.) equaled 20 percent, your employer would deduct $80.00 from your weekly pay of $400.00. This subtraction would leave a net take-home pay of $320.00.

If you figured your tithe on the gross pay of $400.00, it would be $40.00. If you tithed on the net pay of $320.00, it would be $32.00. Notice that the difference is only $8.00.

$10 per hour × 40 hours per week = $400.00 gross pay

Tax at 20% =   − 80.00 tax

                                                    320.00 net pay

Tithe on gross pay of $400.00 = $ 40.00

Tithe on net pay of $320.00 =   32.00

Difference =   8.00 per week

While the difference of $8.00 is not an insignificant amount of money, it is not a tremendous amount either. It's not as if we are talking about a difference of $100.00 per week or more.

Please get this clear in your thinking. In this example, the difference between tithing on the gross and tithing on the net is only about forty minutes of work per week.

Trust in the Lord

Before we go any further, let me interject a verse of Scripture that will help us keep our answer based in God's Word instead of in our own reasoning.

> **Trust in the Lord with all thine heart; and lean not unto thine own understanding.**
> **In all thy ways acknowledge him, and he shall direct thy paths.**
> **Proverbs 3:5,6**

Here God warns us not to try to figure things out through our own foolish wisdom. He tells us to seek our answers from Him.

Put the Tithe First

Notice how specific God is in answering our question about whether or not we should pay the tithe first.

> **Honor the Lord with thy substance, and with the *firstfruits of all thine increase.***
> **Proverbs 3:9**

When you calculate your tithe, start by adding up everything God has graciously given you since the last time you tithed. The sum of these things equals the amount of your increase. According to the verse we just read, the first thing that should come out of your increase is your tithe. By paying God first, you actually honor him with the firstfruits of your increase.

When you pay your tithe first, get ready for a pleasant surprise. It will amaze you when you see what God does for your remaining money. It will go farther than the original 100 percent would have gone. The reason is that God will rebuke the devourer and remove the curse from your remaining 90 percent.

> **Bring ye all the tithes into the storehouse . . . and prove me now herewith. . . .**
> **And *I will rebuke the devourer* for your sakes, and he shall not destroy the fruits of your ground; neither shall your vine cast her fruit before the time in the field, saith the Lord of hosts.**
> **Malachi 3:10,11**

With this fact in mind, let's read the discourse from Proverbs 3 again.

> **Honor the Lord with thy substance, and with the firstfruits of all thine increase.**
> *So shall thy barns be filled with plenty,* **and thy presses shall burst out with new wine.**
> **Proverbs 3:10**

God promises that if you present the tithe first, you will have plenty left over.

God or Caesar

Think about it. Will you put Caesar first by tithing after your taxes are deducted, or will you put God first by tithing before taxes? This decision is not a new one. Jesus faced this same question during His earthly ministry. The Pharisees tried to trip Him up by asking Him:

> **Tell us therefore, What thinkest thou? Is it lawful to give tribute unto Caesar, or not?**

Not only did our Lord's answer startle them, but it also established the biblical priority forever.

> **. . . Jesus perceived their wickedness, and said, Why tempt ye me, ye hypocrites?**
> **Show me the tribute money. And they brought unto him a penny.**
> **And he saith unto them, Whose is this image and superscription?**
> **They say unto him, Caesar's. Then saith he unto them, Render therefore unto Caesar the things which are Caesar's; and unto God the things that are God's.**
> **Matthew 22:17-21**

Please be careful how you interpret what Jesus answered, for some mistakenly think His words mean we should pay Caesar first. However, that is not at all what He said. Jesus would never make a statement that refutes Scripture. His words were always in harmony with the written Word, for He was the Word made flesh.

This is what our Lord was saying, "If Caesar has tax money coming to him, pay it, for we must render unto Caesar that which is due him. We must also give God what is due Him."

United States Citizens Have It Easy

In the United States, our government declares that we are to put God first. Our money boldly bears these words: "In God We Trust." Beyond that, the tax laws of our nation consider our giving to God to be tax deductible. Uncle Sam says you may subtract your giving before you calculate your income tax.

Don't lose sight of this important fact. If you insist on paying the tithe only on your net income, you will end up having to pay a larger amount of taxes to the government.

Sanctified Money

After over thirty years of ministry and Bible study, I am convinced that *tithing on the gross sanctifies your entire paycheck.*

> **For if the firstfruit be holy, the lump is also holy. . . .**
> **Romans 11:16**

When you tithe on the gross (firstfruits of your increase), the remainder of your income becomes holy. It becomes sanctified money. Every Christian knows that sanctified money will always go farther than unsanctified money.

Those who lean to their own understanding may go on tithing on their net income. However, those who do only as "thus saith the Lord" will tithe on their gross income. When they do, they will see their barns filled with plenty.

How do I give a proper offering?

In my speaking engagements around the country, I often ask my audience, "How many of you know how to give a proper biblical offering?"

Their response to that question has been surprising. Very few Christians have any specific Bible information about giving an acceptable offering.

When I speak of an *acceptable offering,* I am not using those words loosely. Your offering must be accepted by God before He is obligated to multiply it back to you.

The Bible says some specific things regarding how to give offerings that are pleasing in the sight of God. According to God's Word, certain ingredients must be present in an offering in order to meet His specifications.

Accepted Offerings

First, God doesn't accept everything Christians place in the offering plate. Now don't misunderstand. Your local church or the ministry to which you give may accept it, but remember that churches and religious organizations don't promise to increase your offerings. Only God speaks of multiplying your offering back to you. His Word does not obligate Him to do so unless He first accepts it.

The Condition of Your Heart

Keep in mind that God is not nearly so interested in the size of your offering as He is in the condition of your heart. Please notice that when Jesus watched the people putting their offerings into the treasury, He did not focus on the amounts they gave. He closely watched *how* they gave their offerings.

> And Jesus sat over against the treasury, and beheld *how the people cast money* into the treasury....
> **Mark 12:41**

We can also see in the words of the Apostle Paul that God looks upon the heart of the giver. When he took an offering for the Church at Jerusalem, Paul said:

> For if there be first *a willing mind,* it [an offering] is accepted according to that a man hath, and not according to that he hath not.
> **2 Corinthians 8:12**

Notice that this verse plainly says the Lord accepts the offerings of those who are of *a willing mind.* If you are willing, you will place no obstacles before your giving.

Some Are Not Willing

Some folks actually put up walls in their hearts that keep them from giving when God speaks. They come to church with the predetermined decision that they are not going to give to certain projects, or that they will give only a certain amount and not a penny more. Many of these people will actually go so far as to leave their checkbooks at home so that there will be no possibility that the moving of the Holy Spirit will sway them at offering time.

God will never accept the offerings of these unwilling minds. The Scripture says He responds favorably to a willing and cheerful heart.

> **Every man according as he purposeth in his heart, so let him give; not grudgingly, or of necessity: for God loveth a cheerful giver.**
> **2 Corinthians 9:7**

Knowing that God loves the cheerful giver, it should become easy to allow your giving to be spontaneous — the kind of giving that comes from a heart full of love. Your attitude should be, "Lord, I see what you've done for me. Now, it's offering time, and look at what I'm going to do for you."

Giving With Gratitude

In order for God to accept your offering, you must not only give it with a willing heart, but also *in accordance* with what you possess.

> **. . . it is accepted *according to that a man hath*, and not according to that he hath not.**
> **2 Corinthians 8:12**

This verse is not saying that your offering is accepted only if it is given *out of* what you already have. If God accepted an offering only if it were given out of what you have, He would not accept a pledge, for a pledge is something you do not yet have.

Please notice the words *according to*. They mean *"based upon."* God accepts your offering if you give it *based upon* (or in accordance with) those things He has already given you. God does not accept your offering if you give it based upon the things you do not yet have.

You should always give your offering *in gratitude for what you have already received from God.* You should never determine the amount of your gift by the fear of insufficiency. Don't focus on what is still lacking in your life. The motivation for a proper offering always comes from a realization of the goodness of God in what He has already manifested in your life.

If you choose the amount of your offering based upon the things you do not have, you are likely to hold back. In effect, you will be penalizing God for that which you don't have instead of blessing Him for what He has done.

God does not cause your lack. Don't penalize Him for it. God will cause you to overcome your lack.

Don't make the mistake of letting what you don't have hinder you from giving generously to your God, or He will reject your offering. When you meet God's scriptural requirements in giving, you can, with confidence, know He has accepted your offering.

How You Feel About It

Secondly, your offering should express the feelings in your heart.

It is important to understand this powerful biblical principle. Whatever moves you, also moves the Lord. In the same way, whatever fails to move you, won't move God.

**. . . we have not an high priest which cannot
be touched with the feeling of our infirmities. . . .
Hebrews 4:15**

A hundred dollar bill does not impress God any more than a one dollar bill. A billion dollars is of no more significance to Him than a penny. How in the world could the God who owns the whole earth be impressed with the value of money? There is only one possible way to impress God with the value of money. He will have whatever feeling you have about it.

Each time you prepare to give an offering, take time to reflect on the amount of the gift you are about to give. Be certain it is an amount that projects your gratitude. Before you release the money, be sure it is enough to convey your innermost feelings.

Remember, $100.00 can be an enormous gift to someone who earns minimum wage, but it may be meaningless to someone who has thousands. If your offering doesn't stir emotions inside of you, don't expect it to touch the Lord's heart. *If your offering is insignificant to you, it will be insignificant to God.*

You can be sure that when your giving produces an emotional response within you, it will produce a personal response from our Lord.

**And there came a certain poor widow, and
she threw in two mites, which make a farthing.
And he called unto him his disciples, and
saith unto them, Verily I say unto you, That this**

> **poor widow hath cast more in, than all they
> which have cast into the treasury:**
>
> **For all they did cast in of their abundance;
> but she of her want did cast in all that she had,
> even all her living.**
>
> Mark 12:42-44

Give for the Right Reason

Thirdly, you must give your offering to accomplish God's purpose. Over the years, I have noticed that much of the money Christians give into the ministry has a selfish motive attached to it. It is easy to deceive yourself when you give. That is why you must be careful not to attach strings to your offerings.

You should give every offering to accomplish God's intended purpose, and not your own. The purpose for your offering should not be to build a tennis court so that you can have a less expensive place to play tennis, or to build a new church camp so that you can save money on your vacation costs. These may be God-ordained projects, but if your motive in giving is to benefit yourself, God will not accept your offering. To give a proper offering, you must never give it for your own benefit. You must always give it to fulfill God's objectives.

God's Purpose Is Clear

The Lord is asking us to follow His simple plan. Look closely at what God is telling us in the following verses.

> **For whosoever shall call upon the name of
> the Lord shall be saved.**
>
> **How then shall they call on him in whom
> they have not believed? and how shall they**

believe in him of whom they have not heard? and
how shall they hear without a preacher?
And how shall they preach, except they be
sent? ...
Romans 10:13-15

God's plan is to evangelize the world. That is His purpose. Next time the offering plate is passed your way, make sure your giving is in line with His agenda. As Romans 10:15 says, we should give so that we can send those who preach.

Harvest Size Is Established

Fourth, your offering establishes your future harvests. Always keep in mind that when you give to God, a double blessing takes place. First, you fund God's purpose. Secondly, your harvest is set in motion.

Remember, the law of the harvest never fails to reward the sower.

... He which soweth sparingly shall reap
also sparingly; and he which soweth bountifully
shall reap also bountifully.
2 Corinthians 9:6

Money given to God always becomes seed in His sight. It takes on the explosive potential of harvest.

If you are a part of a good, soul-winning church, take every opportunity to sow into that good soil. When your favorite Bible teacher blesses you with the Word of God, by all means, sow into that good ground. As Christian television reaches out to your community, bless that station with your offerings. Every time you plant your money in good ground, you are planting a seed that will bring forth a future harvest.

Give With Confidence of a Harvest

Be certain of your harvest by giving in such a way that you meet God's requirements:

1. You must have a willing heart. What God has done for you should motivate your giving.

2. Be sure you attach your emotions and feelings to your offerings. Remember, if it is insignificant to you, it will be insignificant to God.

3. Always give into God-ordained projects that honor Christ. Never give to accomplish your own purpose.

4. When you have done these things, your offering will become seed that will surely bring forth a bountiful harvest.

Why do some people with money hold back in their giving to God?

If the Lord suddenly blessed you with unlimited finances, what would you do with the money? Would you become a great supporter of God's work, or would you keep most of it for yourself?

It may come as a surprise, but many of the wealthiest Christians are actually stingy when it comes to giving to the Lord. No doubt, time will reveal that some people with money who call themselves Christians have never really been born again. They might show an interest in feeding the hungry or clothing the naked. They might even give something toward the church building program. However, many of them finance only that which brings them glory or allows them a nice tax break.

Money Can Be a Barometer

Most people never realize it, but what we do with our money is a barometer of our spiritual life.

> **For where your treasure is, there will your heart be also.**
> **Matthew 6:21**

Wealthy people can use their money to do many wonderful things that exalt our Lord and Savior Jesus

Christ. However, many, if not most of them, never really glorify God with their substance. Money actually causes some to have a false sense of security that eventually leads them to depend upon their wealth rather than on their Lord. This dependence upon money is the reason so few get saved from the ranks of the rich.

> **For ye see your calling, brethren, how that not many wise men after the flesh, not many mighty, not many noble, are called.**
> **1 Corinthians 1:26**

Paul's observation is still true today. Not many wealthy or powerful people are turning their lives to the Lord, much less their wealth. In over thirty years of ministry, I have noticed that a few prosperous people are saved. However, the majority of people who receive salvation are those who are barely getting by.

Some Are Ignorant

Many ask the question, "What about the wealthy Christian who refuses to support God's work? Is he really saved?"

Be careful not to make a hasty judgment on that question. Some wealthy Christians may have only a limited knowledge of what the Bible actually teaches about their financial responsibility to God. The reason for this is that many churches are reluctant to teach what the Scriptures say about money.

Don't misunderstand. The preacher will mention money when there is a building program or a special stewardship campaign. However, the people do not receive regular teaching about finances.

> **My people are destroyed for lack of knowledge. . . .**
> **Hosea 4:6**

Ignorance has caused many wealthy Christians to feel that tithing would erode their wealth. Their lack of biblical knowledge has left them with the mistaken idea that tithing will cause them to lose money.

Knowledge of Scripture will end ignorance. Good Bible teaching on finances will quickly convince most people that giving to God actually increases their wealth! Even more than that, such teaching shows them that giving to God helps shield their wealth from the things that would try to deplete it.

> **And I [God] will rebuke the devourer for your sakes, and he shall not destroy the fruits of your ground; neither shall your vine cast her fruit before the time in the field, saith the Lord of hosts.**
> **Malachi 3:11**

Some people mistakenly believe their money is their own. They look upon tithes and offerings as an unfruitful tax that preachers try to levy against their wealth. These folks don't know that not giving properly to God sets them on the road to poverty.

> **. . . there is [a person] that withholdeth more than is meet, but *it tendeth to poverty.***
> **Proverbs 11:24**

I am convinced that if the men of God would consistently teach what God's Word says about getting money *to* their people — rather than teaching about finances only when they need to get money *from* their people — there would be more than enough money available to meet the need of every Christian endeavor.

Times of Insufficiency Affect Us

I have observed something else about Christians who have money, but do not give. The problem with some of them is not that they don't love the Lord. It goes much deeper than that. Their inability to give goes back to a time of deep poverty in their past. During that time of scant rations, they failed to support God's work. They lived through a time when their personal needs were so great, they did not feel they could afford to give.

These folks may have experienced tremendous financial pressures while they were getting an education or building a business. Perhaps an economic reversal brought them to the brink of bankruptcy. Maybe they had more children than their income seemed able to support. They could have faced any number of possible hardships that caused them to feel they could not give.

Their problem with giving probably wasn't evident to them when it first started. It manifested itself only after they came out of their poverty. Hear the Word of the Lord as He explains the principle they put into motion by not giving when they had little.

**He that is faithful in that which is least is
faithful also in much: and *he that is unjust in the
least is unjust also in much.***
Luke 16:10

Give, Even If It Hurts

Please hear me on this matter. It is of the utmost importance that you establish and maintain a pattern of giving when you go through hard times. You must keep on giving, even if that which you present to God is meager. For the Word of God says that if you are not able to give when you have little, you will not be able to give when you have much.

I thank God every day that my wife and I made it a practice to give when we had virtually nothing. I remember the times we shared groceries with those in need when our own table was almost bare. Because we were faithful when we had little, we have no problem giving to God today.

Child of God, you must make it a practice to tithe and support God's work, even when your own supply is short. In tight times, don't be tight-fisted with the Lord, for the spirit of stinginess will take hold of you, and it will not let go when times get better.

Cast Off the Spirit of Stinginess

If you have failed to give to the Lord in past times of shortage, don't despair. You can still overcome the spirit of stinginess that came with that type of behavior. Confess to God your past inconsistency in giving. Firmly rebuke the spirit of stinginess. Do this by boldly speaking that it must leave. When you speak to it, use the name of Jesus, for every knee must bow to His name.

> **. . . at the name of Jesus every knee should bow, of things in heaven, and things in earth, and things under the earth.**
> **Philippians 2:10**

Then ask God to forgive you. Promise Him you will start giving as often and as much as you can.

God knows the longing of your heart. He will give you deliverance from the spirit of stinginess or any other spirit which takes hold of you. With deliverance will come a fresh, new start.

Question 6

Is it all right for me to give my tithe to the poor?

"Our church has plenty, Brother John," wrote a lady from Wisconsin. "Wouldn't it be okay with God if I just gave my tithes directly to the poor?"

Let me begin to answer this question by saying that where you present the tithe to God is not at your discretion. Scripture is clear regarding this matter. You are to give the tithe to the house of the Lord.

Now, before some of you get upset with me, let's examine the biblical reasons for making this statement. Look again at Malachi 3:10:

> Bring ye *all* the tithes into the storehouse....
> Malachi 3:10

Please notice the word *all*. You are to use no part of the tithe for such things as educating your children, making personal trips to the mission field, or to buying blankets for the homeless. The Word of God says we must bring *all* the tithe into God's storehouse.

Where is the storehouse of God today? Malachi 3:10 says that when the tithe is brought to the storehouse, there will be meat in *God's house*.

41

> **Bring ye all the tithes into** *the storehouse,*
> **that there may be meat in** *mine house.* **. . .**
> **Malachi 3:10**

The storehouse is clearly God's house. Compare this statement with the Word of God from the Book of Timothy.

> **. . . that thou mayest know how thou**
> **oughtest to behave thyself in the** *house of God,*
> *which is the church* **of the living God, the pillar**
> **and ground of the truth.**
> **1 Timothy 3:15**

There it is in black and white. The church is the house of God.

Two things about the tithe never change.
1. The tithe is always *10 percent.*
2. The tithe always goes to *God's house.*

Scripture establishes those two constants.

Lending to God

You may have never before heard what I am about to say. When you give to the poor, God does not look upon your gift as being a tithe, a seed, or an offering. God looks upon your giving to the poor as a personal loan to Himself.

> **He that hath pity upon the poor** *lendeth unto*
> *the Lord;* **and that which he hath given will he pay**
> **him again.**
> **Proverbs 19:17**

Contributing to the poor is completely different from the types of giving with which most Christians are familiar.

In fact, it is not even giving. Contrary to most teaching, it does not carry with it the promise of a multiplied return to the giver.

Think this thought through with me. When a person takes out a legitimate loan, he doesn't have to pay it back at enormous interest rates such as 30, 60, or 100 percent. Many people repay the exact amount that they borrowed, especially when they receive the loan from a friend. God's Word says not to charge usury from a brother. (See Deuteronomy 23:19.)

The Tithe Is Not a Loan

When you feel led to give to the poor, God looks upon your giving as a loan. He takes on the personal responsibility of seeing to it that you receive back what you have given.

The tithe is totally different. It is not a loan from you to God. The tithe is the Lord's property. According to Scripture, it never belonged to you in the first place.

**And all the tithe of the land, whether of the
seed of the land, or of the fruit of the tree, is the
Lord's: it is holy unto the Lord.
Leviticus 27:30**

Now don't misunderstand. Your church may decide to use a part of your tithe to help the poor. However, it is not to go directly from your hand to the hand of the poor. You must first place it into the house of God, for the tithe belongs to God.

Don't Turn a Deaf Ear

In no way am I encouraging you to turn a deaf ear to those in need. Don't be like the man who came to me after a recent meeting and said, "I'm never going to give to the poor again. From now on, I'm going to give only where I can get a good harvest!"

I immediately warned him to take heed of what God says in Proverbs 21 before he put his plan into action.

> **Whoso stoppeth his ears at the cry of the poor, he also shall cry himself, but shall not be heard.**
> **Proverbs 21:13**

If you turn a deaf ear to the destitute, God says He will someday turn a deaf ear to your cry for help. Don't invite unnecessary problems into your life. Always be generous with your offerings to those in need.

God Promises Unending Opportunity

Sharing with the poor is clearly very important to God, for He said we would always have an opportunity to do so.

> **For ye have the poor with you always, and whensoever ye will ye may do them good. . . .**
> **Mark 14:7**

We find this practice of lending to God through giving to the poor throughout Scripture.

> **But whoso hath this world's good, and seeth his brother have need, and shutteth up his**

**bowels of compassion from him, how dwelleth the
love of God in him?**
1 John 3:17

It is proper to feel compassion for the poor. However, you must keep in mind that the tithe should never become *designated giving.* Always do the scriptural thing, and let the church decide what to do with your tithe.

Can you give your tithe to the poor instead of to the local church? The Word of God says no!

Is it right to pay the tithe first when I have bills I have promised to pay?

When I talk about putting the tithe above everything else a person owes, many Christians become upset with me. They say, "Brother John, how can God expect me to tithe? I don't even have enough money to pay my bills. God must know I have signed legal contracts. I'm sure He wants me to have a good testimony, and to do that, I must pay my bills on time!"

Robbing Peter to Pay Paul

Perhaps we should approach this question a little differently. Would it be all right for you to skip the house payment because the car payment was due? You may say, "Why, that would be foolish, Brother John. I have an obligation to both of them, and as an honest Christian, I have to pay all of my bills."

That's right. It wouldn't be right to pay one and not pay the other.

When you begin to understand what God's Word actually says about tithing, your view of this whole situation will drastically change. You will realize it is just as wrong to say no to God as it is to say no to the landlord, car payment, or utility bills.

Whom Did You Owe First?

There is no question about it. All Christians have a moral and scriptural obligation to pay the bills they owe, but let's get our priorities straight. Long before you ever talked about buying a house, purchasing a car, or turning on the lights, God had established a valid claim on 10 percent of your income. He clearly stated that it belonged to Him.

> . . . all the tithe of the land, whether of the seed of the land, or of the fruit of the tree, is the Lord's: it is holy unto the Lord.
> And if a man will at all redeem ought of his tithes, he shall add thereto the fifth part thereof.
> Leviticus 27:30,31

Notice that God looks at your tithe as a bill you owe Him. He charges a late fee if you don't bring it to Him on time. Why, God's late fee on the tithe is much stiffer than the late fees on any of the other bills you agreed to pay. He charges 20 percent. It sounds as if God believes your tithe belongs to Him, and He expects to get it on time.

"Well, Brother John, why should I pay attention to that? Isn't God a loving God? Surely He won't hurt me for not tithing."

You had better pay attention to what the Word of God says. If you don't tithe, you hurt yourself, for the windows of heaven close over non-tithers. How will you ever pay off that mountain of bills you owe if your heaven is closed? Your health, job security, even the tires on your car, all need the blessing of God that He gives to those who live under an open heaven.

Don't Make the Big Mistake

It is a big mistake to believe you must pay your bills first, and then if there is anything left over, pay your tithes last. God established His instructions to tithe at the foundation of the earth.

God expected Adam and Eve to tithe. If you remember, it was their job to take care of all of the trees in the garden. However, God did not allow them to eat from one particular tree. They bestowed their labor on it, but they could not eat of its fruit. It was their tithe to God.

God expected Cain and Abel to tithe. The Bible tells us that Abel brought *the firstlings and the best of his flock.* That was the first and the best of his increase, or his tithe.

God Has First Claim

God has always had first claim on man's income. His claim began with the first man, Adam, and it continues today. Let there be no confusion as to which obligation you should pay first. God's instructions are clear on this matter.

Honor the Lord with thy substance, *and*
with the firstfruits of all thine increase.
Proverbs 3:9

God says to *pay Him first* out of what He has placed in your hands. When you do, your health and your entire life will be blessed and peaceful.

> My son, forget not my law; but let thine
> heart keep my commandments:
> For *length of days,* and *long life,* and *peace,*
> shall they add to thee.
> Proverbs 3:1,2

Don't follow the path of reason, for it will keep the benefits of an open heaven away from you!

Give God That Which Is His

When He told the Pharisees to give Caesar the things which are Caesar's, and to give God the things which are God's (Matthew 22:21), Jesus gave a tremendous word of clarification on this subject. We are to give to the landlord the things that are his, not the things which are God's. We are to give to the power company the things which belong to the power company, not the things which are God's. We are to give to the automobile financing institution the things that are theirs, not the things which are God's.

Even though you may have made purchases on credit, you must never forget that before you give Caesar what is his, you must first render unto God that which is His. He says *the firstfruits belong to Him.*

I cannot tell you which bill you should pay after you pay the tithe. The rent, the car note, the phone bill—you will have to decide that for yourself. However, I can say on the authority of God's Word that you should pay the tithe first, for it is to be the firstfruits of all your increase.

The Greatest Claim

Thousands of people in the Church don't tithe because they don't understand their relationship to the

One who has given them life. God has a greater claim on your finances than anyone. His claim is greater than any bill you owe, for He is your Creator, Savior, King, and Lord!

Which obligation should you pay first? By all means, it should be your tithe!

Question 8

Should I give to the Lord if my husband doesn't want me to?

In the past several years, people have asked me this question dozens of times. "Should I pay tithes if my husband doesn't want me to? Should I give offerings if my spouse has told me not to do it?"

Let's look at first things first. A proper biblical marriage is one in which the couple bases important decisions on God's Word and then mutually agrees upon them. A marriage based in Christ is more than a relationship in which one partner dominates the other.

Strange as it may seem, the only Bible verse that some husbands seem to know is, "Wives, submit yourselves unto your own husbands . . . ." (Ephesians 5:22).

Please note that the verse just before this one is equally as important. It says husbands and wives should submit themselves "one to another in the fear of God." (See Ephesians 5:21.)

There is a big difference between a husband who is the head of his home and one who is the dictator of the home. The scriptural job of the husband is not shouting orders to his wife like a military general. If he is a biblical husband, he will not rule with an iron fist. He will operate in great love and will allow the Scripture and the Holy Spirit to guide him.

The Head and the Heart

Someone gave me some real wisdom several years ago. That person told me a husband should, indeed, be the *head* of the home. However, for that home to operate properly, his wife should be the *heart* of the home. When you find a combination like that in a marriage, you have found a rock-solid home. It will be heaven on earth.

Proper Husbands Are Not Terrors

As the leader in the home, the husband should avoid being a terror to any good work his wife or children might perform.

> **For rulers are not a terror to good works, but to the evil. . . .**
> **Romans 13:3**

There is no question that tithing is a good work. Giving to God is always a good work. Feeding the hungry or sheltering the homeless is a good work. If he wants to exercise biblical authority in household matters, a man will never rebel against doing what is good and right in God's sight.

Time and time again I see wives who love the Lord, are active in their churches, and have powerful Christian testimonies. However, they cannot give to God because their husbands won't allow it. The Word of God warns those husbands not to be a terror to good works in their homes. Proper husbands should do everything in their power to promote tithing and giving offerings.

Let Your Wife Help You

How wonderful it would be if these rebellious men would realize that their godly wives can help them stay out of trouble. Let me tell you about a woman of the Old Testament who saved her husband's life by doing God's will. She was Zipporah, the wife of Moses.

The Scripture tells us that God was ready to release Israel from Egyptian captivity. Moses was His chosen man to bring about their deliverance. However, Moses had left one important matter undone. He had never circumcised his son.

On the way from Midian to Egypt to deliver the children of God from bondage, the Lord spoke to Moses and told him he would soon die if he didn't immediately circumcise his son.

> **And it came to pass by the way in the inn,
> that the Lord met him, and sought to kill him.**
> **Exodus 4:24**

For some unexplained reason, Moses hesitated in doing what God had clearly commanded. Thank God for his obedient wife, for she stepped in and circumcised the boy herself.

> **Then Zipporah took a sharp stone, and cut
> off the foreskin of her son. . . .**
> **Exodus 4:25**

Let me speak a word of wisdom to the husband who doesn't have a heart for tithing. I strongly recommend that you allow your wife to lead you in this good work. Her obedience to God's Word in this matter may be the only thing that will keep you from being laid off your job. It may even be that the open heaven which your tithe would cause will someday allow the healing power of God to save your physical life.

There May Be an Alternative

If you cannot reach a compromise, and your husband continues to say no to your tithing and giving of offerings, don't give up hope. There may be an alternative. You may consider tithing on whatever household funds you have in your control. If you work outside your home and earn your own paycheck, you should be able to tithe on it.

Keep a list of God's blessings, and when you have established a track record of the miracle-working power of the Lord in stretching the money you tithe on, show your husband the goodness of God. Surely when he sees how God's hand has moved on your behalf, he will change his decision and allow you to give the Lord what is rightfully His.

The Power of Two

Always do your best to have total agreement in your home. A husband and wife will see the best results when they are in agreement. Remember, one can chase a thousand, and two will put ten thousand to flight. (See Deuteronomy 32:30.)

Share with your husband how powerful agreement can be. Show him from the Bible what Jesus said about it.

> . . . **if two of you shall agree on earth as**
> **touching any thing that they shall ask, it shall be**
> **done for them of my Father which is in heaven.**
> **Matthew 18:19**

If your husband has never given his heart to Christ, pray fervently for his salvation. Your fervent, effectual prayers will accomplish a great deal.

> . . . **The effectual fervent prayer of a**
> **righteous man availeth much.**
> **James 5:16**

If you and your husband have both confessed Christ as your Lord and Savior, and your husband still won't allow you to tithe, here is my recommendation. Have a serious discussion with him concerning what kind of marriage he envisions. Is it a Christian marriage, one that is being led by the Bible? Does he understand what the Bible means when it tells both husband and wife to *submit to each other?* Does he believe a marriage should be filled with mutual respect and loving negotiations and compromises? When it comes to giving to God, is he leading the family with good ideas, or is he basing his decisions on God's own Word?

Every wife should have the right to ask for clarity on these matters. Do you have a *Christian marriage* or a *heathen marriage?*

If you cannot reach a compromise, *do not tithe or give offerings behind your husband's back.* You should lovingly and respectfully keep the issue before him. Bring it up to him as often as possible.

Whatever you do, don't give up. Remember, it takes patience as well as faith to obtain God's best.

> . . . be . . . followers of them who through
> faith and patience inherit the promises.
> **Hebrews 6:12**

Question 9

Do I have to catch up all of my unpaid, back tithes in order to be right with God?

The question of *back tithes* gnaws at the consciences of many Christians. Those who gave their hearts to Christ as children and have always obeyed the Lord in tithing have no cause for concern. However, what about the person who was saved as an adult? What about his earnings of all those years before he started tithing? Does God require that he pay those back tithes?

The 20 Percent Penalty

We have already discussed the Word of God in Leviticus 27:13 regarding the Lord's demand of 20 percent interest on unpaid tithes. (See Question 7.) Does that mean you must add 20 percent to all your unpaid tithes and immediately pay the whole amount in order to be right with God?

Those who have studied the issue generally agree that God does not require New Testament saints to catch up their back tithe. The born again are not commanded to look at their past years of income, add 20 percent, and pay the total.

This conclusion has a biblical basis. Look closely at this often-quoted verse.

> **Bring ye all the tithes into the storehouse, that there may be meat in mine house, and prove me now herewith, saith the Lord of hosts, if I will not open you the windows of heaven, and pour you out a blessing. . . .**
> **Malachi 3:10**

God simply states that if we begin to tithe faithfully, He opens heaven over our lives. He doesn't say anything about our having to catch up everything from the past. The Lord asks only that we begin, and He reinstates our open heaven.

Provision and Protection

Every Christian needs to know that God has presented a clear plan regarding paying the tithe. When we violate that plan, we sin. God even identifies the kind of sin we commit. He calls it "God robbing."

> **Will a man rob God? Yet ye have robbed me. But ye say, Wherein have we robbed thee? In tithes and offerings.**
> **Malachi 3:8**

As we all should know, the blood of Christ washed away our sins. At the time of our new birth, we became new creatures in Christ. However, for many people, a year or more may have passed before they began to tithe. Others may tithe only sporadically, and some may have stopped tithing altogether.

When God gave His Son as the ultimate remedy for sin, He also made Jesus our ongoing advocate (lawyer) to help us gain forgiveness for any sins we might commit after salvation.

> **. . . if any man sin, we have an advocate with**
> **the Father, Jesus Christ the righteous.**
> **1 John 2:1**

The Bible says we are saved by grace. However, if we occasionally fail to obey God's instructions, Jesus will plead our case with the Father to obtain our forgiveness.

I hope you will get this knowledge into your spirit. If you belong to the Lord, you should be a tither. Tithing is one of His clear commands to you as His child. If for some reason you have failed to tithe, you must immediately begin anew. Start tithing today. Just as surely as God forgives any other sin, He will forgive all the back tithe and open the windows of heaven over you. He promises to extend a helping hand to those who have drifted away from tithing.

> **. . . Return unto me, and I will return unto**
> **you, saith the Lord of hosts. . . .**
> **Malachi 3:7**

In the same way that He made provision for our other transgressions, God has made a way back for the one who has robbed Him of the tithe.

Get Into a Good Church

Be sure you attend a church where you will get the whole counsel of God. Many Christians do not receive proper teaching in the ways of God. Some churches teach only a limited gospel. The message of salvation is wonderful, but some pastors rarely preach anything else.

Christians also need to hear about sanctification, justification, discipleship, the second coming of Jesus, the doctrines of faith, and the deity of Christ. They should also receive regular, in-depth teaching on biblical economics.

I hope your church teaches the whole counsel of God. However, if it doesn't, and no church near you does, get some reliable books on biblical economics and study them. As an obedient believer, tithing should be an uncompromised part of your daily walk.

Do unpaid back tithes have to be caught up? No. God has made provision to cancel all past-due tithes automatically, and to rebuke the devourer. Once you begin to tithe faithfully, He marks your account *paid in full* and opens the windows of heaven, freely releasing His abundant blessings.

If you are not a faithful tither, start tithing today. Watch how quickly things change for the better in your life when you live under an open heaven.

The Bible says we are not supposed to be the borrowers, so why is there a mortgage on my church?

Many Christians are puzzled about church mortgages, especially when they read God's promise that they are to be the lenders and not the borrowers.

> . . . thou shalt *lend* unto many nations, and thou shalt *not borrow.*
>
> Deuteronomy 28:12

"If that scripture is true, why is my church strapped with building payments?" asked a viewer of our television program.

Like Begets Like

Let me begin by saying that no God-called pastor carries a note on the building because he *prefers* a mortgage to a debt-free church. I have never met a preacher who pled with his congregation, "Please don't pay off the church mortgage. Let's stay in debt so that we can pay all of our money in interest instead of using it to win the lost."

We need to understand that church mortgages exist because of certain biblical principles. The first one is the principle that like always begets like.

Apple trees bring forth apples, and watermelon seeds will produce watermelons. Genesis records that at the time of creation, God programmed all the creatures to bring forth only after their own kind.

> **And God said, Let the earth bring forth the living creature after his kind, cattle, and creeping thing, and beast of the earth after his kind: and it was so.**
> **Genesis 1:24**

This same principle is also at work in other realms. A person who is friendly attracts friends (Proverbs 18:24). The law of the harvest declares we will reap what we sow (Galatians 6:7).

Mortgaged Houses Cause Mortgaged Churches

You may wonder what all of this has to do with your church mortgage. People who live in mortgaged houses, drive mortgaged cars, and live up to their eyeballs in debt, will usually cause the institutions that serve them (churches, schools, etc.) to have mortgages as well. It works like the domino effect. Their debt impacts every aspect of their lives.

In a community where nearly all the people are in debt, the city will have to issue bonds (debt) to build new schools, roads, and utilities. Their industries will have to borrow in order to do business.

Here is the bottom line. If mortgaged people make up the membership of an organization, that organization will usually carry a mortgage on its physical facility (lands, buildings, equipment).

On the other hand, institutions in areas where the population is essentially debt free are usually also debt free.

The same principle works with churches. If they have mortgages on their homes, most of the members are going to use the greater part of their cash for paying their lenders instead of helping their church pay off its mortgage.

Let me say it another way. People who live in debt will probably belong to churches that are also in debt.

The Church Is a Body

In addition to the law of like begets like, there is another reason that churches have monthly payments. As believers, we are not many bodies, but we are *many members of one body.* Read what Paul wrote to the church at Corinth:

> **For as the body is one, and hath many members, and all the members of that one body, being many, are one body: so also is Christ.**
> **1 Corinthians 12:12**

When the church doors open, with our natural eyes we see many bodies, or people. However, when the Lord looks into the church, He sees all of the people as if they were one person. Let's read the rest of what Paul said:

> **And whether one member suffer, all the members suffer with it; or one member be honored, all the members rejoice with it.**
> **1 Corinthians 12:26**

When we consider this verse, it should come as no surprise to find that the church as a whole will be just as the members are. The way in which the members purchase their real estate, automobiles, business equipment, and so on, will be the same way in which the church purchases those items.

I am aware that there are exceptions to every rule, but most churches will mirror the financial philosophy of the majority of their members.

How to Pay Off the Church

How do we get our churches out of debt? One pastor approached the situation like this. He said, "I'm going to ask my people to take out second mortgages on their homes and give the proceeds to the church so that we can pay off the church debt."

I couldn't help but discourage this action. I said, "Pastor, stop and think. What would that program really accomplish? The debt burden would still be on the body. The money of your people would still be going to interest instead of to the great commission."

After many years of seeking a workable solution to the problem of church debt, God has led me to this conclusion. The best way to cancel the debt of a church is to concentrate on canceling the debts of its members.

My prayer is that every pastor throughout the world will put into practice the following words. Dear Pastor, if you want your church building out of debt, *get your individual church members out of debt.* Focus on getting the Smiths, the Johnsons, and everyone else mortgage free, and then just watch the principles of the Word go to work and quickly remove your church debt.

Knowing that whatsoever good thing any man
doeth, the same shall he receive of the Lord....
Ephesians 6:8

You will find that whatever happens to the majority of the members of the church will also happen to the church corporation. If you have worldly members, you will have a worldly church. If you have spiritual members, you will have a spiritual church. If you have debt-free members, you will have a debt-free church.

Churches have mortgages because their members have mortgages.

Question 11

Is it right for ministers of the gospel to have a better-than-average lifestyle?

In recent years the media has persistently bombarded the nation with so-called exposés about ministers of the gospel that they feel are experiencing too much of the good life. These reports have caused uninformed Christians to question whether or not the men and women of God — apostles, prophets, evangelists, pastors, and teachers — should receive more than just an average wage.

Let me begin by saying I am in no way defending the financial abuse of which some are guilty. However, when I answer a question about the proper lifestyle for God's ministers, I am duty-bound to do so according to the Word of God.

Tradition and God's Word Differ

Most people are amazed when they find that the Scripture addresses the issue far differently from how they would imagine.

Traditionally, most people believe the lifestyle of a minister of the gospel should be average, or probably even below average. Many Christians and non-Christians alike hold this view. However, God's Word doesn't tell it that way.

One of the hardest things to accept is that God's Word on this subject will probably not make much difference to many folks because of their traditional beliefs.

> . . . ye made the commandment of God of
> none effect by your tradition.
> **Matthew 15:6**

If we are to have God's mind about the lifestyle of His ministers, it is evident that we will have to go beyond the traditions of man.

Double Pay for the Men and Women of God

It is interesting to read what the Bible has to say about how the Church is to pay its ministers. It's much different from the traditional view.

> Let the elders that rule well be counted
> worthy of *double honor,* especially they who labor
> in the word and doctrine.
> For the scripture saith, Thou shalt not
> muzzle the ox that treadeth out the corn. And,
> The laborer is worthy of his reward.
> **1 Timothy 5:17,18**

The Word of God clearly states that ministers are to receive double honor. The word *honor* doesn't mean we are simply to open the car door for Pastor or take off our hats in his presence. The word *honor* speaks of the money he is to receive for his labor among us. The Bible is talking about how much we should pay our spiritual leaders. Those who labor in the Word and doctrine should receive at least *double pay.*

Notice that after saying that ministers should receive double pay, Paul backed up his statement by quoting from the Old Testament.

> **Thou shalt not muzzle the ox when he treadeth out the corn.**
> **Deuteronomy 25:4**

Then, he further emphasized his statement by quoting the words of Jesus. These words clearly spoke of wages.

> **. . . the laborer is worthy of his hire. . . .**
> **Luke 10:7**

Only the spiritually blind could miss the fact that Paul was speaking of financial remuneration!

The Blind Cannot Lead the Blind

Satan wants to keep the Church from grasping this truth. He knows exactly what will happen when we financially bless the ministers of the gospel. When he leads a better-than-average lifestyle, a pastor will be able to lead his congregation into a better-than-average lifestyle. The devil would rather see your pastor live in need, never realizing the prosperity God promises. Satan knows that if the blind leads the blind, they will both end up in a ditch. He also knows if a poor man leads poor people, they will all stay in poverty.

> **. . . if the blind lead the blind, both shall fall into the ditch.**
> **Matthew 15:14**

This truth operates between a pastor and his congregation at every possible level. If the pastor has never been baptized in water, chances are no one in his congregation will ever be baptized. If the pastor is not born again, there is a big chance that nobody else in his church will find the Lord. You see, a pastor can't lead his people where he has not been.

This truth operated in my own life. For fully half the years of my ministry, I did not believe God gave the gifts of the Holy Spirit to us today. During that time, I never brought even one of my church members into the fullness of the Holy Spirit. It was not until I personally experienced His fullness that I was able to bring it to the members of my church.

How does that truth relate to your pastor's lifestyle? If he walks in constant shortage, he will not be able to lead his congregation into biblical abundance.

Being Average Is Not God's Best

Someone told me a long time ago that *average is twice as good as the worst, and half as good as the best.* If he is ever going to lead you into God's best, your man of God must first experience the best. If he has to live his whole life with average or below-average finances, most of his congregation will have to live there with him. If your pastor is not well paid, it is unlikely that he will be able to lead you into God's abundance.

Allow your man of God to move up financially. Let him live in a nice house. It won't hurt him to have a good, new car. New clothes will not corrupt him and his family. Think about it. Will he be a better person if you keep him in an old car and used clothes? I think not.

Lift up your voice so that other members of your church can hear you. Let them know that you feel Pastor should have extra funds to take his family on special vacations. Encourage them to help you financially bless him. When they do this, a church will immediately see a dramatic change in the financial condition of family after family in the congregation.

Keep God's leader in abundance, and he will be much better qualified to lead his people into God's abundance. Remember, your man of God cannot take the congregation into spiritual dimensions he has not experienced.

Should the men and women of God have better-than-average lifestyles? Tradition says no. The Word of God says yes.

Question 12

Is it all right to make a pledge to God if you don't have the money in hand when you make it?

The biblical concept of vows and pledges has stirred up the church of our day. Even with everything people are teaching about it, most folks are not searching the Word of God for the truth.

At the outset of this discussion, let me say that pledges and vows are biblical ways of giving. Just because we don't totally understand something is not a good reason to judge it as unscriptural. The Bible contains several different kinds of pledges, vows, and pacts that God not only honors, but actually promotes.

A Faith Promise

One type of pledge or vow is commonly called a "faith promise." This is a promise to give a certain thing or amount by faith. The person who makes a faith promise asks God to provide the thing he wishes to give. This type of pledge is a special blessing to those who don't have the funds they would like to give.

A faith promise is the type of pledge Hannah made when she asked God for a son.

> **And she vowed a vow, and said, O Lord of hosts, if thou wilt indeed look on the affliction of thine handmaid, and remember me, and not forget thine handmaid, but wilt give unto thine handmaid a man child, then I will give him unto the Lord all the days of his life. . . .**
> **1 Samuel 1:11**

By using a faith promise, people who would never be able to give any sizeable amounts of money to God can get started doing so. Here is an example of how it works.

Suppose you desire to give $1,000.00 into the work of God. However, you don't even have 10 percent of that amount. Don't give up on the idea of giving the $1,000.00. Just use the faith promise form of giving. Pray to God and say, "Lord, you know I don't have $1,000.00, but I believe you can give me $1,000.00. When you do, I promise faithfully to put it into the ministry."

Your first vow of $1,000.00 may seem like a tremendous leap of faith. However, if you just think about it, you will realize it isn't any harder for God to provide $1,000.00 than it would be for Him to provide $1.00.

The hardest part of a faith promise is passing the money on into the ministry after God provides it. You see, producing $1,000.00 takes no special effort on God's part. The only possible problem in the process is getting the $1,000.00 through the person who asked for it and into the hands of the church or ministry to which he promised it.

Faith Promise Turns Into Cash Giving

Today my wife and I are able to give to the Lord in ways we would have thought impossible just a few years ago. When we reviewed our giving at the end of last year, we looked at each other and asked, "How is it possible that we were able to give that much? Why, just a few years ago we were living on less than we now give."

How did we get this situation to take place in our lives? Believe it or not, we started with faith promises. We simply promised God, and then we faithfully kept our promises. As we fulfilled each one, the money we gave became seed. Then that money seed began to multiply. The more we promised and gave, the more we received from God until our cup literally began to run over. If it worked for us, it will work for you.

> ... God is no respecter of persons.
> Acts 10:34

A Conditional Promise

We call another form of pledge or vow a "conditional promise." This is a promise to give a certain thing to the Lord if He meets a certain request. This is the type of vow Jephthah made.

> And Jephthah vowed a vow unto the Lord, and said, If thou shalt without fail deliver the children of Ammon into mine hands,
> Then it shall be, that whatsoever cometh forth of the doors of my house to meet me, when I return in peace from the children of Ammon, shall surely be the Lord's, and I will offer it up for a burnt offering.
> Judges 11:30,31

Jephthah made a conditional vow. He said if the Lord would provide deliverance, he would give Him the first thing that stepped out of his door when he returned home safely.

How could this type of vow apply to you? Let's say you have a piece of land or a house to sell. Your conditional vow might be that if the Lord helps you sell the house, you will give Him an extra 10 percent of your profit. (Please notice that you will also owe a tithe on the profit. You are promising an *additional 10 percent* on the profit when it sells.)

It might work for a farmer like this. He might pray, "God, if you help me have an exceptional harvest this year, I'll put an extra $2,000.00 into the building program at our church."

Another way it could work for you might be this one. Let's say several people are in line for a promotion at your place of employment. You might make the following conditional promise. "Lord, for one year I'll give you half the increase I will receive with the new position if you will help me get the promotion."

These are only a few examples of conditional vows. Once you try this method of pledging and see how effective it is, you will use it again and again.

A Time-Delayed Promise

Another kind of pledge or vow is the "time-delayed promise." Let's say God is directing you to give something, but you don't have it with you. Perhaps you are watching a telethon on a Christian television station, and you feel God wants you to give a certain amount. You call the station; however, you can't hand them the money at that moment. You will have to send it in the mail. So, you promise to mail it the next day.

Notice that your gift won't be given instantly. It will take a few days for it to get to the station. What you have made is a time-delayed promise.

Maybe you want to give a certain amount, but the money is in your savings account. You promise it, but you can't actually give it until you go to the bank and make a withdrawal. This is the same thing. It's a time-delayed promise.

A Word of Warning

There is always a danger when a person makes pledges or vows. Many times a person will make a vow, and then he will forget all about it and never fulfill the promise. Forgetting pledges is easy since most Christian ministries do not send collection letters.

Hear God's Word on this important subject.

> **When thou vowest a vow unto God, defer not to pay it; for he hath no pleasure in fools: pay that which thou hast vowed.**
> **Better is it that thou shouldest not vow, than that thou shouldest vow and not pay.**
> **Ecclesiastes 5:4,5**

Some people read this scripture and understand it to say we should never make vows to God. That conclusion is wrong, and it will rob you of the blessing that proper pledging brings to the child of God.

The Way to Make Vows Work

There is a way to make a pledge and not miss the mark. Don't wait until you have the entire amount you pledged before you give. Start giving toward your vow as soon as possible. Give the first extra money you get as partial payment of your pledge. If you keep up this process, before long you will have paid the entire amount.

If you make a faith promise, a conditional promise, or a time-delayed promise, the most important thing is to make it with a pure and honest heart before God. If you do, God will always help you fulfill your promise.

Is it all right to make a pledge to God if you don't have the money when you make it? The answer is yes. It is all right to make a pledge. However, it is not all right to make a promise to God and then not pay it.

Question 13

Does the Bible say God's children should never borrow money?

"Brother John, the Bible clearly states that we are to 'owe no man anything.' Does that mean I should never take out a loan?"

I have received many letters asking this question. Basing your understanding of God's Word on just one verse can be a dangerous way of interpreting Scripture. To keep from misinterpretation, it is important to see each individual verse in its immediate context, as well as in the context of the whole Bible. This is one reason that God's Word calls for two or three witnesses to establish truth.

> . . . In the mouth of two or three witnesses
> shall every word be established.
> **2 Corinthians 13:1**

Here is a perfect illustration of the importance of this principle. A few years ago, the Lord instructed me to wage the *war on debt*. I have no doubt that He spoke this command into my heart. However, I would never have been able to follow His leading successfully if I had based the whole strategy on just a few words from part of one verse. Before we can establish biblical doctrine, we must be sure we have a full picture of what God is saying.

Keep Things in Context

Many people are concerned with the five-word statement from the Book of Romans, "Owe no man any thing." Please notice that these five words are only part of the verse. Romans 13:8 actually has nineteen words, and beyond that, there are fourteen verses in the chapter.

To understand properly what the apostle was saying with those five words, we must look at the complete verse and the verses that surround it. That is where we will find the biblical context of the words, "Owe no man any thing." Pay close attention to the verse immediately before this one.

> Render therefore to all their dues: tribute to
> whom tribute is due; custom to whom custom;
> fear to whom fear; honor to whom honor.
> **Romans 13:7**

Upon close examination, we find that the command from verse 8 to owe no man anything has to do with rendering honor to whom honor is due, taxes to whom taxes are due, and customs (import/export tariffs) to whom they are due. These scriptures are speaking of our relationship with the governing authorities and our speedy payment of taxes and customs. It is not a command never to borrow.

Good Men Borrow

A verse from the Book of Psalms applies to our discussion. It is what I call a neglected verse. For some reason, nobody ever uses it when discussing the biblical principle of borrowing. As you read it, notice that it speaks

of the difference between a good man's attitude toward
the lender and the evil man's attitude.

**Evil men borrow and "cannot pay it back"!
But the good man returns what he owes with
some extra besides.**
Psalm 37:21 TLB

Before we read that we are to "owe no man any thing,"
and then decide that God's Word tells us we should never
borrow, let's realize that God's Word also says, ". . . the
good man returns what he owes. . . ." This verse clearly
implies that the good man borrowed something.

The Bible and Borrowing

The Old Testament is specific about lending and
borrowing. For example, it says not to lend for extremely
long periods of time. Israelites were not to charge one
another interest. Every seven years and every fifty years,
they were to cancel all debts.

God gave special laws about borrowing oxen and
borrowing grinding stones. There were even rules about
collateral and how the lender was to hold it. For instance,
if you took a man's blanket as collateral, you had to return
it to him each night so that he wouldn't be too cold. You
couldn't totally take away a person's grinding stone or one
of his vital farm instruments. If a man used his millstone
as collateral, God's law required you to return it to him
when he needed to grind meal.

It is obvious that God understood people would have
to borrow from time to time, or He would never have
addressed the subject so extensively. Nowhere in

Scripture does God absolutely prohibit the borrowing of money!

A Season Is Appointed to Everything

Solomon gave some sound advice we can apply to borrowing.

> **To every thing there is a season, and a time to every purpose under the heaven:**
> **A time to be born, and a time to die; a time to plant, and a time to pluck up that which is planted.**
>
> **Ecclesiastes 3:1,2**

Solomon said our lives should have cycles of events and activities. For example, you should not stretch out the payments on your house so that it takes all your life to pay it off. If you have to borrow when you buy a home, you should set aside a reasonable season of time to pay for it.

Most people make the mistake of paying the smallest payment possible when they borrow. Worse than that, many people attempt to borrow the greatest amount they possibly can for the longest period of time they can. They do so, usually because they fall into the trap of multiple debts. *Multiple debts come from borrowing to purchase everything* from vacuum cleaners to vacations. Before long, these people lose control of their finances, and they find themselves literally fulfilling the Word that says:

> **. . . the borrower is servant to the lender.**
> **Proverbs 22:7**

Don't Encumber That Which Belongs to God

You should always remember that when you are in debt, you are no longer your own. If the Lord were to inspire you to give a large gift to a ministry, and you were up to your eyeballs in debt, you would not be able to give it. As long as you owed that money, your allegiance would have to remain divided. You would have to say no to God and yes to the creditor, for your debt would make you the servant of the lender.

Debt not only makes you the servant of the lender, but also constantly prohibits you from being everything God wants you to be.

Does the Bible say God's children should never borrow? No, it doesn't say that. However, it does warn us against a lifestyle that keeps us continually burdened with financial obligations.

Question 14

Is it wrong for Christians to use credit cards?

If you look back through history, you will find that the greater part of the Church has opposed almost every new concept or invention to come along. When I first entered the ministry, I was amazed when I read some of the sermons that had been preached around the turn of the century. Of all things, some ministers had preached against automobiles. They said cars were instruments of the devil sent for no other reason than to scare the horses. This mentality still prevails today among some people. It is common knowledge that the Amish people still hesitate to ride in mechanically powered vehicles.

When radio came along, you would have thought Satan himself had arrived. Preachers began to say the prince and power of the air was the radio (Ephesians 2:2). Movies were even worse. Surely they were the mark of the beast (Revelation 19:20). With the advent of television, many preachers immediately renamed it the *hellevision*.

Without even putting up a fight, we literally handed over to Satan the mass media and modern communications! Instead of rushing in and taking the radio frequencies for our Lord, we left them for the world to take. Instead of seeing the potential for motion pictures to present the gospel story, we handed them over to

Hollywood without any opposition. If Christians had applied for television channels when they were virtually free, we would now dominate that most powerful media. Instead, we must spend millions to buy just a few channels back from the devil's crowd.

Many years ago when I became born again, very few people ever placed personal checks in the offering plate. I can remember when offerings were mostly cash. Christians usually didn't give checks to the church. They prided themselves on using only *real money.*

Personal checks were new, so the Church was against them. Some thought they might even be the mark of the beast. However, if you were to look at an offering today, you would find that most of it is usually in the form of personal checks.

An Electronic Check

Amazingly, the Church today has that same old mentality about credit cards. Folks constantly ask me if it is wrong for Christians to use them.

First of all, let me make one clarification. Banks don't actually issue credit cards. They issue *bank cards.* Their users turn them into credit cards when they decide not to pay them off at the end of each month.

I believe with all of my heart that a plastic bank card is nothing more than an electronic check. Instead of writing out a personal check on a piece of paper, we use a plastic bank card to write out an *electronic check.* This practice is not evil. It simply transfers funds electronically from the bank of the giver to the bank of the receiver.

Bank Cards Help Win the Lost

Bank cards (credit cards) have helped greatly in world evangelism. Many Christian ministers who share the gospel around the world would not be able to do so if they had to carry cash. I cannot imagine how I would safely carry enough currency to take care of my needs for thirty days in Australia, Africa, or Asia. Once the word got out that I was carrying cash, the crooks would say, "Here comes Avanzini," and there would go my money. If it weren't for bank cards, I would have to hire a full-time security guard to protect me from being robbed.

I believe evaluating bank cards is easy. If people use them correctly, they will be a blessing. If they misuse them, they will become a curse.

Bad Checks Hurt the Gospel

You may not realize that people can abuse personal checks just as easily as they can abuse bank cards. Our ministry accepts cash, personal checks, or bank cards at our book table. When a person pays us with a bank card, we can process the transaction immediately and receive approval or disapproval as to whether or not the person has funds to cover his purchase. Because of this ability, we don't usually lose any money on bank card sales.

However, personal checks are a totally different story. We regularly receive and deposit checks that the bank returns to us marked "insufficient funds." Then we not only have lost the price of the books, but also must pay a fee for processing the bad check.

Sometimes a bank will return a check to us indicating that the account has been closed for six months. Sometimes we even receive checks back from a bank with a notation that no such account ever existed! The truth is, bad checks hurt ministries financially more often than bank cards do.

Use Your Bank Card Properly

There is nothing wrong with using your bank card as an electronic check. Just pay off the balance at the end of each month. Never use a bank card as a quick loan. If you do, you will soon be paying 18 to 20 percent interest on the balance.

Scripture tells us to:

> **Let all things be done decently and in order.**
> **1 Corinthians 14:40**

It is not decent, nor is it orderly behavior to pile up debts on a credit card. Such a practice can lead only to disaster. Never forget what Jesus said:

> **For which of you, intending to build a tower,**
> **sitteth not down first, and counteth the cost,**
> **whether he have sufficient to finish it?**
> **Luke 14:28**

God wants you to be responsible in your use of money, even when you spend it in the form of a bank card.

Is it all right for Christians to use credit cards (bank cards)? The answer is yes. Should Christians misuse credit cards? The answer is no. We should use credit cards only for one purpose, to transfer funds electronically.

Is it all right to co-sign a loan for a friend or family member?

How would you respond if one of your friends or relatives called and said, "I have a big favor to ask. The bank will give me a loan of $5,000.00 to start my new business if I have a co-signer. Will you co-sign the note for me?"

On the surface it sounds so simple. You don't have to put up any money. You won't be making the payments, and, best of all, you will be blessing a friend. You answer, "Sure. I'll be glad to sign for you."

Before you sign your name on the dotted line, you need to consider a few facts. First, co-signing gives you all the liabilities of a loan without any of its benefits. The lending institution always gives the money to the person requesting the funds, not to the co-signer. Then, if your friend fails to make the monthly payments, the responsibility of making them falls squarely on your shoulders.

The Bank Probably Knows Best

Many people fail to realize that when the bank requires a co-signer, it is a clear signal. They have determined that your friend or relative *is not likely to pay the money back.* Keep in mind, the bank made its decision based on an extensive investigation of your friend's credit report. They checked his qualifications for running the business he proposes to start, and they have checked his income potential and expenses.

Remember, the bank wants to loan money. That's how they make their money. So if they have turned down your friend, it is for a number of good reasons.

When he told your friend or relative he needed a co-signer, in essence the banker was saying, "Bring us someone who qualifies to pay back this loan, and we will lend the money." This fact will become evident to you when the bank insists on examining *your* credit record. They will require *you* to be credit worthy before they will allow you to co-sign. They will base their decision to loan the money to your friend solely on *your own* ability to pay them back. Make no mistake about it. The bank will look to *you* for payment.

You May Need a Loan

Another reason to think twice about co-signing a loan is the possibility that an emergency or an opportunity may arise, and you may need to borrow some money yourself. The banking community may not want to lend you any money if you have co-signed for someone else, for until your friend has repaid that loan, the bank considers it to be *your loan*.

I recommend that you pause a moment before co-signing for anyone. Consider carefully what you have just learned. Are you really better qualified than the bank to judge the credit worthiness of your neighbor? Have you

ever seen his credit report? Is it worth losing your money
as well as your friendship if he fails to repay?

A Case When Co-signing Might Work

There is one circumstance when co-signing might be
beneficial. If someone already owes you money and is not
paying you back, you might consider going to the bank with
him and helping him take out a loan *so that he can repay
you* with the money. Make it clear that you will co-sign the
loan, but he will be responsible for every payment. Let him
know this will give him a chance to build up some good
credit. Then, from the very first month, you must become
personally involved with seeing to it that he pays each
payment on time.

Please note: *Do not spend the money from the loan
until your friend has repaid the bank.* If for some reason he
defaults on the note, you will have to use the money he
borrowed from the bank to pay it off yourself.

This plan is only a suggestion and will not work in
every instance.

The Word of God Speaks

Let's now turn to the Bible for some input. What does
it have to say about co-signing?

> **My son, if thou be surety for thy friend, if
> thou hast stricken thy hand with a stranger,**
> **Thou art snared with the words of thy
> mouth, thou art taken with the words of thy
> mouth.**
>
> **Proverbs 6:1,2**

Surety means "to guarantee against loss, or to be a co-signer." If you co-sign the note, the Word of God says you have become caught in a trap, or snared. Hear yet another verse of warning against co-signing.

> **A man void of understanding striketh hands, and becometh surety in the presence of his friend.**
> **Proverbs 17:18**

The Bible says co-signers don't have any understanding. This statement makes it clear that it is better not to be a co-signer.

Those Who Are Caught

I can hear some say, "Good advice, Brother John, but what about me? I've already co-signed a note for someone. Does the Bible have any instruction for me?"

Yes, the Bible also answers that question. After warning against becoming surety for your friend, the Bible goes on to say:

> **Do this now, my son, and deliver thyself, when thou art come into the hand of thy friend; go, humble thyself, and make sure thy friend.**
> **Proverbs 6:3**

Go to the person with whom you have co-signed and say, "You know I am concerned about your well being. It must be evident, because I co-signed your note to help you get the loan you needed. However, I didn't go far enough. I don't want you ever to need a co-signer again, so I personally want to help you manage your finances."

In effect, you are becoming his financial advisor. Offer to meet with him weekly or monthly. Make sure you schedule your meetings on the day he receives his paycheck. Diligently help him plan and maintain his budget. Continue to emphasize that your goal is to help him so that he will not need a co-signer in the future. Then be sure to guide him in his budgeting so that there are always funds available each month to make the payment on the loan you have co-signed.

The Bible says clearly that you should not waste any time getting this program started.

> **Give not sleep to thine eyes, nor slumber to thine eyelids.**
> **Deliver thyself as a roe from the hand of the hunter, and as a bird from the hand of the fowler.**
> **Proverbs 6:4,5**

Don't let another day go by until you have addressed the issue. The Word says you are like a deer in the cross hairs of the hunter's rifle when you have co-signed a loan. Move quickly to release yourself from this jeopardy.

Should you co-sign for a friend or relative? The Bible says an emphatic no!

Question 16

Is it wrong for a divorced Christian to avoid paying legal child support?

"The courts have ordered my former husband to pay child support," wrote a lady from Los Angeles. "He calls himself a Christian, yet he doesn't send the money. Does the Bible say anything about his responsibility?"

Let me begin by saying my answer will not be a discussion of whether or not divorce is right. We will be talking about the economic dilemma that many Christians face by either paying or trying to collect child support.

I will be addressing this question with some first-hand knowledge, for divorce has touched some of my own children. With each of those divorces came the problem of either paying or collecting court-ordered, child support payments.

Impossible Demands

Sometimes the law can seem unfair when it comes to child support. I have known fathers that the courts ordered to pay child support every month, yet they allowed them to see their children only two or three times a year. The law ruled that some fathers had to pay the support, and *never* allowed them to see their children!

In some cases, the court imposed financial demands that were nearly impossible to pay. I know of a father who did not contest the divorce. He agreed to every demand. Then the court issued him an order for a monthly payment amount which has now become impossible for him to pay, because his circumstances changed drastically. He was in the construction industry and earned large sums of money for a long period of time. Then a sudden downturn to the economy brought the building industry to a stop. This father is now on unemployment, but his child support payment has remained the same.

We could go on indefinitely, discussing the unfairness of the system to the father. However, we must also understand the tremendous difficulty the mother and children may face if they don't receive their monthly support.

Think of Your Children

The children of the marriage did not cause the divorce, and they should not have to suffer because of their parents' decision. So often the divorced father adds to his children's confusion and misery by his lack of financial support. His unscriptural behavior causes the mother and children to live in constant insufficiency.

Day after day their mother must say things such as, "No, we can't afford to buy you new shoes. No, we can't go to McDonald's tonight. Daddy didn't send the check."

It's difficult for children to believe that God the Father is their heavenly provider when their own earthly father fails to provide for them.

Look to the Word of God

Let's go beyond these circumstances and see what the Bible has to say about child support. To begin with, it tells us to obey the laws of our land.

Put them in mind to . . . obey magistrates. . . .
Titus 3:1

We are to obey the magistrates, or those who legislate our laws. Please don't misunderstand. This verse doesn't mean we can't appeal unfair legal decisions. However, keep in mind that until a legal court order lowers your support payment, the law requires you to pay it. Court-appointed child support is not optional for the Christian. The Word of God instructs him to obey the law.

The Bible also says we who are believers have an obligation to support our children.

But if any provide not for his own, and
specially for those of his own house, he hath
denied the faith, and is worse than an infidel.
1 Timothy 5:8

The Bible plainly says the person who does not provide for the children he brought into the world has "denied the faith." Scripture declares such a person to be worse than an unbeliever, or an infidel. It further says:

And, ye fathers, provoke not your children
to wrath: but bring them up in the nurture and
admonition of the Lord.
Ephesians 6:4

Some fathers may say, "Well, Brother John, I don't get to bring them up anymore since the divorce took place, so I don't feel I should have to pay."

That's no excuse! Even after the divorce you are to care for them to the best of your ability, or you are worse than an infidel.

Some Godly Advice

I have some advice for those who pay child support. It may someday make all the difference in the world to your relationship with your children.

If I were paying child support, I would make every check out to my former spouse and clearly write the names of my children in the memo section of the check. I would write a personal letter to the children, make a photocopy of it, and mail the original letter along with the check each month.

After the bank returned the check to me, I would photocopy both sides. I would neatly arrange the photocopies of each check and every letter in a scrapbook. Along with those two items, I would also keep a record of every visit I had with my children.

Then, if they ever asked, "Daddy, why didn't you love us and care for us?" or said, "Mother said you never sent any money to help us out after you and she were divorced," I could show them the scrapbook. I could tell them that even though I couldn't always do everything I wanted to do for them, I always did everything I was able to do.

You Have a Responsibility

Is it wrong for a divorced Christian not to pay legal child support? Yes, it's wrong. No matter how unfair you may think the judge has been, it is your obligation. Regardless of how your former spouse may be spending that money, you must financially support your children, and thereby show them your love.

Hopefully a day will come when you can sit down with your children and show them that even though the court didn't allow you to spend every day with them, you were still a good Christian and did what the Word of God commanded you to do.

For those mothers who struggle to collect child support, please know that as I have written this chapter, I have been praying for you. If your children's father is a Christian and still won't pay, send him a copy of this book. Ask him to read this chapter. It is possible that the Holy Spirit will convict him concerning his God-ordained responsibility to his children. I pray that when he reads it, he will start doing that which is right in the eyes of God.

Question 17

Is filing bankruptcy immoral
or unscriptural?

With legal bankruptcy at an all-time high, an ever-increasing number of Christians are writing and asking, "Brother John, is it a sin for a Christian to file bankruptcy? Does the Bible teach against it? Is it immoral?"

Please don't think I am trying to escape the issue by giving you these two answers. However, they are both correct.

1. Yes, filing bankruptcy is an unscriptural action.

2. No, taking bankruptcy is not an unscriptural action.

Unscriptural Bankruptcy

Let's look first at when bankruptcy would be unscriptural. It would always be unscriptural behavior to file bankruptcy for the sole reason of not paying your bills. God's Word tells us we are to be honest in business matters. Christians, of all people, are not to defraud their fellow man. Paul clearly stated this principle to church leaders.

> Moreover he must have a good report of them which are without. . . .
> 1 Timothy 3:7

We need to have a good record, both inside and *outside the church*. The community should have confidence that we are honest people.

Let me say again, if you file bankruptcy simply to avoid paying your bills, it is wrong.

The Origin of Bankruptcy Law

Contrary to common belief, modern-day bankruptcy law does not find its origin in man's system. U.S. Bankruptcy law came to us by way of British Jurisprudence (law), which bases its bankruptcy law on a principle found in the Holy Bible.

The bankruptcy codes of today are rooted in Leviticus 25. A close reading of that chapter will reveal two special processes that God instituted and made a part of the Mosaic Law.

The Seven-Year Release

One of those ordinances was *the seven-year law of release*. The law automatically cancelled all debts at the end of every seven years. No matter how large or small they were, the law permanently cancelled every liability at that time.

God did not establish this law because He wanted to be unfair to the creditor, for any lender who had any sense at all would simply not issue a loan for longer than seven years.

This release had two positive effects. It kept the nation from long-term borrowing, and it took care of uncontrollable debts. If a man owed money after the seven-year period had passed, this rule automatically cancelled his debt.

Please notice that this law wasn't for the purpose of allowing deadbeats to get out of paying their legal obligations. God designed this law for a totally different reason. It was a merciful way of releasing those who just could not pay. It also showed the creditor exactly how to handle the debt of someone who experienced an unforeseen tragedy.

The Jubilee

The second ordinance was called *the year of jubilee*. It took place after seven cycles of seven years (49 years). The people would hold a special celebration in the fiftieth year, and they would release every debt and obligation. This release was so complete that the original owner would receive back every piece of property he had ever owned.

**In the year of this jubilee ye shall return
every man unto his possession.
Leviticus 25:13**

Christians should realize that the bankruptcy law is not a tricky, legal maneuver to avoid paying bills. When a person approaches it in honor and righteousness, it is a form of God's grace extended to the business affairs of His children. Bankruptcy comes from a foundational truth found in Scripture, and it exists for our benefit.

Scriptural Bankruptcy

With this said, maybe now you will understand why I must say that in certain circumstances, bankruptcy can be both scriptural and moral. Extreme disability is a good example.

How do you treat the debts of a man who is suddenly involved in a horrible accident? Suppose his spinal cord is severed, and he is in a coma. He no longer has the ability to earn a living. Since he did not get into that accident to keep from paying his bills, releasing him from his debts would be the only Christian thing to do.

What about a wife whose husband suddenly deserts her, leaving her with a houseful of children? Suppose he goes to another state and she can't locate him or make him pay child support. The bills he ran up before he left were in both their names. Now, the collectors are knocking at her door. Her only outlet may be to say, "It's out of control. I have to file bankruptcy, for there is no way I can pay these bills and still feed my children."

The same problem can occur if the wife deserts the husband. I know of a man whose wife ran up enormous credit card bills. Then she left him holding a financial bagful of unpaid debts which he could not pay. After looking at all of his options, he had no choice but to file for bankruptcy.

What about the victims of natural disasters such as earthquakes, floods, or hurricanes? What if a disaster suddenly destroys a new home, but the mortgage is still due?

Think about it. Legitimate circumstances can arise when there is no foreseeable way of financial recovery. Should the law require a person to pay and pay until he and his family are utterly destroyed?

When there is no way to pay a debt, when every cent a person can earn won't be enough to pay the bill, God's Word says, "Release him!"

Please hear me on this point. I am not suggesting that bankruptcy is a biblical way to avoid paying your legal debts. Instead, we should view it only as a merciful release for those who, because of uncontrollable circumstances, have no possible hope of ever paying back what they owe.

A Word to the Lender

If you are a lender faced with a loss through a properly motivated bankruptcy, let your attitude toward the debtor be tempered with compassion. When you are dealing with people in the dire straits of financial collapse, ask yourself what the Lord would do in this situation. Instead of trying to get blood out of a turnip by extracting every penny you have coming, remember there may come a day when you are totally unable to pay what you owe. The Word of God promises that the mercy you show now, may be shown to you later.

> **And as ye would that men should do to you, do ye also to them likewise.**
> **Luke 6:31**

> **. . . whatsoever a man soweth, that shall he also reap.**
> **Galatians 6:7**

Let me say again that I am not advocating bankruptcy. However, I do believe that in certain situations, God approves of the process.

Bankruptcy can be either moral or immoral, scriptural or unscriptural, according to the reason behind it.

Is it all right for a Christian to save money?

Recently I received this question in the mail. "The Bible says we are to take care of the poor and hungry, and we should also give generously to evangelize the world. Does that mean Christians should give away everything and never put any of their money in a savings account?"

In my travels around the country, I have found that people hold a wide variety of views on this topic. One man I highly respect told me, "Brother John, I believe if I have a penny left in the bank when the Lord returns, it will prove I have been a total failure." He felt he should put all of his extra money into the work of God.

Base Your Life on God's Protection

One of the first things we need to understand is that Christians should base their lives on faith in God. For our very existence we depend on God and His ability to supply for us. His provision and protection should be the cornerstone of every Christian's financial plan.

David had this type of faith, for he clearly recognized God as his source in the Book of Psalms.

The Lord is my shepherd; I shall not want.

He maketh me to lie down in green pastures: he leadeth me beside the still waters.

He restoreth my soul: he leadeth me in the paths of righteousness for his name's sake.

Yea, though I walk through the valley of the shadow of death, I will fear no evil: for thou art with me; thy rod and thy staff they comfort me.

Thou preparest a table before me in the presence of mine enemies: thou anointest my head with oil; my cup runneth over.

Surely goodness and mercy shall follow me all the days of my life: and I will dwell in the house of the Lord for ever.

Psalm 23

We must recognize God as our source just as David did. God is the one who meets our needs.

Fear of Economic Collapse

People have many reasons for questioning whether or not they should be saving any money. Some ask out of fear, "What about the coming economic crash? What will happen when my money is not worth the paper it's printed on? What if the government fails? Please help, Brother John! What can I do to protect myself?"

If you have faith in God, you don't need to worry about what is going to happen to our society. It doesn't have to be the end of your world if the stock market crashes. Whether interest rates rise or fall, your lifestyle shouldn't fluctuate to any great extent if God is really your source.

Savings Accounts Are Scriptural

Let me go on to say that it is both scriptural and responsible for Christians to have some money set aside.

The Bible specifically states that God's children are to have savings.

> **Blessed shall be thy basket and thy store.**
> **Deuteronomy 28:5**

The *basket* speaks of your daily needs. The *store* speaks of your savings, or that which is placed in your storehouse.

Scripture also tells us that a good man will leave an inheritance to two generations.

> **A good man leaveth an inheritance to his**
> **children's children: and the wealth of the sinner**
> **is laid up for the just.**
> **Proverbs 13:22**

From this verse you can see that we should make some kind of financial provision for our offspring. This proverb makes it clear that God expects us to have savings.

Savings, not Treasure

Now, please notice I said *savings.* There is a marked distinction *between savings and treasure.* When he speaks of his treasure, a person is talking about his most valued possessions. However, when you operate in true biblical economics, you must see yourself as the *steward over God's possessions.* Your earthly belongings are not your own. If you are God's steward, everything you have belongs to Him. It is impossible for a true steward to have earthly treasure!

Consider this lesson from the ant about planning for the future.

> **Go to the ant, thou sluggard; consider her**
> **ways, and be wise:**
> **Which having no guide, overseer, or ruler,**
> **Provideth her meat in the summer, and**
> **gathereth her food in the harvest.**
> **Proverbs 6:6-8**

The ant shows us the wisdom of setting something aside for the future. However, just as surely as we can have a wise attitude toward our savings, we can also be foolish in this matter. Think about the story of the rich farmer who operated his savings plan in such a way that God Himself ended up calling him a "fool."

> **. . . The ground of a certain rich man**
> **brought forth plentifully:**
> **And he thought within himself, saying,**
> **What shall I do, because I have no room where to**
> **bestow my fruits?**
> **And he said, This will I do: I will pull down**
> **my barns, and build greater; and there will I**
> **bestow all my fruits and my goods.**
> **And I will say to my soul, Soul, thou hast**
> **much goods laid up for many years; take thine**
> **ease, eat, drink, and be merry.**
> **Luke 12:16-19**

This man's mistake was in putting his soulish nature in charge of his savings. The one who chooses to put his soul in charge of the important decisions of his life will never have the right attitude toward his savings. Your decisions must come from your redeemed spirit, not from your soul. If you walk a spirit-led life, you will please God. If you walk a soul-led life, God will call you a "fool," for only a fool would lay up treasure for himself and not be rich toward God.

But God said unto him, Thou fool. . . .
So is he that layeth up treasure for himself,
and is not rich toward God.
Luke 12:20,21

Christian Stewards, Take Note

As a Christian steward, I believe it is wise to hold a reasonable amount of funds in reserve. It should be an amount you consider to be prudent in relation to your responsibilities.

In our own ministry, we have a number of employees. I would be irresponsible if I were to spend every dime that comes in. God demands that I keep a reasonable surplus in store, for several families derive their livelihood from our ministry.

If you are the head of a family, the same policy should apply. I'm not saying you should try to save enough money to cover everything that could ever go wrong. It would be impossible for anyone to do that. The foundation stone of your savings plan should always be your dependency upon God to provide. If your family tithes and gives proper offerings, you will place yourself under the open heaven of God. In that position, God guarantees you protection if the *unforeseen* comes to pass.

Christians should save for the *foreseeable* future. That might include the major purchases every family must make from time to time, educating your children, special desires such as vacations, and, of course, retirement.

The following verse is special to my wife and me. It has helped us so much with making decisions about things for which we cannot find an absolute dollar amount given in God's Word.

> ... let the peace of God rule in your hearts. ...
> **Colossians 3:15**

The word translated *rule* in this verse actually means "umpire." The writer of Colossians was saying, Let the peace of God be the umpire in your decision-making process.

Guideline to Savings

How much savings is enough? Follow these suggestions, and I believe you will be safe. Faithfully tithe, give generously into the Kingdom of God, then seek the guidance of the Holy Spirit as to how much you should set aside. He will give you peace about the correct amount.

Is it all right for Christians to save money? Yes, if they save according to biblical principles, relying on God as the ultimate protector and provider of the family. Remember, God will call you a "fool" if you allow your savings to become your treasure.

Instead, go ahead and set aside a reasonable amount. Then, handle your savings with prudence, wisdom, and responsibility, and God will be sure to bless your storehouse.

Question 19

How is it possible that my giving affects my praying?

When I was a new Christian, I believed my giving and my praying were totally separate activities. Then one day, God opened my eyes to see that *everything* we do for the Lord is linked together.

For many years I agreed with the theologians about prayer. I thought God would either answer a prayer request, or it would go into a golden vial, awaiting the end of time when God would pour it out. (See Revelation 5:8 & 8:4.) While this is what I believed the Bible taught, it surely didn't give me much comfort. However, when I began to understand what the angel told Cornelius in the Book of Acts, I realized there was a third possibility.

Giving and Praying Mixed Together

The story of Cornelius totally changed my perspective. His praying affected his giving, and his giving affected his praying. When he merged together these two activities, it was as if a spiritual explosion took place.

> There was a certain man in Caesarea called Cornelius, a centurion of the band called the Italian band,
>
> A devout man, and one that feared God with all his house, which gave much alms to the people, and prayed to God alway.
>
> He saw in a vision evidently about the ninth hour of the day an angel of God coming in to him, and saying unto him, Cornelius.
>
> And when he looked on him, he was afraid, and said, What is it, Lord? And he said unto him, *Thy prayers and thine alms* are come up for a memorial before God.
>
> Acts 10:1-4

As you can see, Cornelius had been crying out to God. He had also been giving generously. While these two things might have been separate in Cornelius' mind, they surely were not separate in God's mind. The angel told Cornelius that God viewed his praying and giving (alms) as something bigger than praying alone, and bigger than giving alone. They had merged together before God to become a memorial. Read these further words from the Scripture.

> And Cornelius said, Four days ago I was fasting until this hour; and at the ninth hour I prayed in my house, and, behold, a man stood before me in bright clothing,
>
> And said, Cornelius, thy prayer is heard, and thine alms are had in remembrance in the sight of God.
>
> Acts 10:30,31

As a result of his *giving and praying,* his request was permanently suspended in the presence of God. It hung there awaiting God's speedy answer.

The Widow at Zarephath

This same type of thing happened in the Old Testament to the widow in the city of Zarephath. Without a doubt, she was a woman of prayer. The Word says that God spoke audibly to her. (See 1 Kings 17:9.) In the midst of terrible famine, I have no doubt that she prayed to God often about her dwindling barrel of meal. However, as hard as she prayed, nothing happened. Her barrel just kept getting more and more empty.

Then one day she added giving to her praying. When she gave of her food to feed the prophet, God immediately answered her prayer. The moment she joined giving to her prayer, God's hand reached down into her barrel of meal and multiplied it.

It was a miracle answer, for as long as she gave and prayed, God supplied her need.

> . . . she, and he [Elijah], and her house, did eat many days.
> And the barrel of meal wasted not, neither did the cruse of oil fail, according to the word of the Lord, which he spake by Elijah.
> **1 Kings 17:15,16**

Every time she fed the prophet, more meal appeared in the widow's barrel.

The Widow With Two Mites

Because of my Calvinist education, I didn't believe God would still perform miracles in that same way today. However, I couldn't deny the Scripture, for it surely teaches that this type of miracle is available to us. It became more clear when I studied the account of Jesus at

117

the treasury. One day Jesus went into the temple to watch people put their money into the offering box.

> **And there came a certain poor widow, and she threw in two mites, which make a farthing.**
> **And he called unto him his disciples, and saith unto them, Verily I say unto you, That this poor widow hath cast more in, than all they which have cast into the treasury:**
> **For all they did cast in of their abundance; but she *of her want* did cast in all that she had, even all her living.**
> **Mark 12:42-44**

Notice that the Scripture says *the widow gave because of her want.* I cannot overemphasize this fact. She had a definite prayer request attached to her giving. *She wanted something.* When she attached her two mites to her prayer request, she got the attention of Jesus. Here again we see giving and praying mixed together.

As Cornelius, the widow at Zarephath, and this widow with the two mites can testify, when you mix praying and giving together, the whole is greater than either of its two parts. When you link giving and praying together, Scripture says your gift definitely affects your prayer. Together they turn your request into a memorial that stands before God, awaiting His answer.

Question 20

Is there anything wrong
with being rich?

I have been asked this question hundreds of times. "Does the Lord want Christians to be wealthy? Is there anything wrong with being rich?"

Perhaps the best way to answer is to go back to the roots of our faith. As God's children, our roots are not planted in poverty. We did not come forth from people who lived in constant insufficiency. In fact, our spiritual ancestors were people of tremendous wealth.

Our Wealthy Forefathers

What does the Scripture say about the financial condition of our spiritual ancestors? Let's begin where it all started, with Adam and Eve. The Bible says they were rich. God gave them more than just the garden of Eden. The Lord told them to take dominion over the whole earth. (See Genesis 1:28.)

Noah was also rich. With the great flood, he took possession of everything of value on the earth. He took the wealth of the world with him in the ark. I believe I would be safe in saying he was the most prosperous person in the whole world on the day the flood came. (See Genesis 6 & 7.)

When Abraham came out of Egypt, the Bible says he was *very rich.* (See Genesis 13:2.)

Isaac had such large possessions of flocks, herds, and water wells that the Philistines actually envied him. (See Genesis 26:14.)

Jacob also had great possessions, and he recognized that God was the One who had made him rich. (See Genesis 33:5.)

Joseph rode in the second chariot in Egypt and wore the king's ring on his finger. During the world's worst recorded famine, he had control of all the food in the known world. He was obviously wealthy. (See Genesis 41:57.)

King Saul was rich, and so was David. King Solomon was wealthy beyond description. Even the Old Testament prophets had servants who traveled with them.

Was Jesus Poor?

Jesus was prosperous enough to own his own home.[1] When two men asked Him where He lived, He invited them over to spend the night.

> **Then Jesus turned, and saw them following,
> and saith unto them, What seek ye? They said**

---

1   *Please note that when Jesus said, "Foxes have holes, and birds of the air have nests; but the Son of Man hath not where to lay his head" in Luke 9:58, He was not saying He had no house. He was simply stating that He had no place to stay that night, because the Samaritans had cancelled His meeting and refused to give Him lodging.*

unto him, Rabbi, (which is to say, being
interpreted, Master,) where dwellest thou?
   He saith unto them, Come and see. *They
came and saw where he dwelt,* and abode with him
that day: for it was about the tenth hour.
John 1:38,39

It is well-known that Jesus had a treasurer, and He
wouldn't need a treasurer unless He handled large sums
of money. He also wore expensive clothes. The Bible says
His coat was seamless. A seamless garment was the most
expensive and highest quality clothing available.

The apostles had plenty of material wealth. Why else
would Jesus have to tell them not to take any money with
them when they went out on the road? (See Luke 9:3.)

The Apostle Paul was rich enough for a Roman
proctor named Felix to lose his soul trying to get a bribe
from him. (See Acts 24:25,26.)

Both the Old and New Testaments are clear regarding
the financial condition of our forefathers in the faith. They
were people of substance. Then what about you and me?
Does God want His children to be rich today?

The answer to that question is yes. God says financial
riches are a part of His blessings.

The blessing of the Lord, it maketh rich,
and he addeth no sorrow with it.
Proverbs 10:22

The Apostle Paul also declared God's desire for His
children to prosper.

For ye know the grace of our Lord Jesus
Christ, that, though he was rich, yet for your

sakes he became poor,[2] that ye through his
poverty might be rich.

2 Corinthians 8:9

Look further. The Apostle John wrote:

Beloved, I wish [pray] above all things that
thou mayest prosper and be in health, even as
thy soul prospereth.

3 John 2

John's number-one prayer was for you to live in health
and prosperity.

Is there anything wrong with being rich? For some
reason, many religious leaders think there is. However,
according to the Bible, the answer is no. There is nothing
wrong with Christians being rich.

---

2   *Please note that when he spoke of Jesus becoming poor, Paul was
comparing our Lord's wealth in heaven to His wealth on earth. From
the moment Jesus left the splendor of heaven, anything He owned on
earth was poverty by comparison. A paraphrase of 2 Corinthians 8:9
might be: Our Lord Jesus Christ left the glory of the riches of heaven
and entered the poor realm of the inferior riches of earth, that we
might become rich.*

Conclusion

Thank you for considering the answers I have presented in this book. To the best of my knowledge, they are in agreement with the Word of God.

If any of these answers have offended you, I apologize for the discomfort I may have caused. However, I cannot apologize for any discomfort the Holy Spirit may have caused.

If you feel you have a different answer to one or more of these questions, please write and share your biblical view. I would like to hear from you.

I know there are many questions I have not answered. If you have a question I have not dealt with, drop me a line. I will try to get back to you and attempt to give you an answer as soon as I can. You may address your questions and comments to:

**His Image Ministries
Attn: T.L.C. Department
P.O. Box 1057
Hurst, TX 76053**

Let me close with this verse of Scripture. It applies to the answers of theologians, denominations, and critics, as well as to your answers and mine. This verse makes a clear statement to anyone who gives an answer contrary to the Word of God.

**. . . let God be true, but every man a liar. . . .
Romans 3:4**

Other Books by John Avanzini

Always Abounding — Enter a new dimension of abundant living through a plan from God's Word that cannot fail. **$5.95**

Faith Extenders — Study how characters from the Bible caused their faith to grow, and increase your faith. **$7.95**

Financial Excellence — The best of John Avanzini in one special edition. Bonded-leather binding. Gift boxed. **$19.95**

Hundredfold — See clearly and thoroughly the scriptural laws of seed-time and harvest, God's plan for your increase. **$7.95**

It's Not Working, Brother John! — Here is what to do if you've done all you know and still haven't received God's promises. **$8.95**

Moving the Hand of God — Discover how you can get God's attention focused on your most urgent need. **$6.95**

Powerful Principles of Increase — Find out how you can take the resources of this world to establish God's Kingdom. **$8.95**

Stolen Property Returned — Learn how to take the thief to the heavenly courtroom, and recover what he has stolen. **$5.95**

The Wealth of the World — Find help to prepare for your part in the great end-time harvest of souls and wealth. **$6.95**

The Financial Freedom Series

War on Debt — If you are caught in a web of debt, your situation is not hopeless. You can break the power of the spirit of debt. **$7.95**

Rapid Debt-Reduction Strategies — Learn practical ways to pay off all your debts — mortgage included — in record time. **$12.95**

The Victory Book — This workbook takes you step-by-step through "The Master Plan" for paying off every debt. **$14.95**

Have a Good Report — Find out what your credit report says about you, and learn the steps that will help you correct the negative information. **$8.95**

Complete both sides of this order form to receive a 10% discount on your book order!

Qty	Title	Cost	Total
	Always Abounding	5.95	
	Faith Extenders	7.95	
	Financial Excellence	19.95	
	Hundredfold	7.95	
	It's Not Working, Brother John!	8.95	
	John Avanzini Answers Questions	6.95	
	Moving the Hand of God	6.95	
	Powerful Principles of Increase	8.95	
	Stolen Property Returned	5.95	
	The Wealth of the World	6.95	
	War on Debt	7.95	
	Rapid Debt-Reduction Strategies	12.95	
	The Victory Book	14.95	
	Have a Good Report	8.95	
	Subtotal		
	Less 10% Discount		
	Shipping & Handling		2.00
	Total Enclosed		

( ) Enclosed is my check or money order made payable to **HIS Publishing Company**

Please charge my: ( ) Visa ( ) MasterCard

Account #_____

Expiration Date ____ / ____ / ____

Signature_____

To assure prompt and accurate delivery of your order, please take the time to print all information neatly.

Name_____

Address_____

City_____State_____Zip_____

Area Code & Phone (____)_____

Send mail orders to:

HIS Publishing Company
P.O. Box 1096
Hurst, TX 76053